St. Jerome School

Grade

Lesson Plan

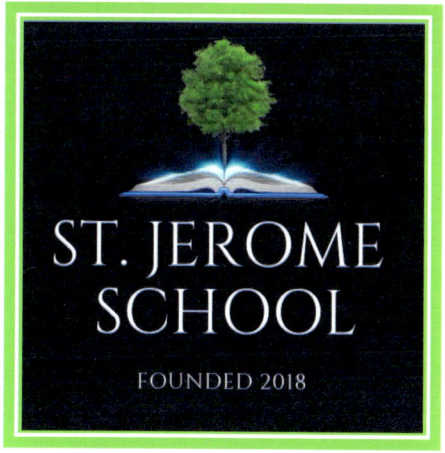

St. Jerome Library
WWW.STJEROMELIBRARY.ORG

COPYRIGHT ©2019AD-2024AD BY ST. JEROME LIBRARY PRESS

FAIRBANKS, INDIANA

ALL RIGHTS RESERVED.

No part of this book may be reproduced or transmitted in any form or by any means, electronic or mechanical, including photocopying, recording, or by any information storage or retrieval system, without written permission from the publisher.

Thank you!

A Word about St. Jerome School

St. Jerome School is a branch of St. Jerome Library, the parent nonprofit organization to our mission of helping Catholic families to homeschool by providing affordable options in the most important vocation of raising saints for heaven. St. Jerome School & Library is a publisher, a true library, a bookstore, and a school, in the sense of providing teaching materials and lesson plans.

We use a simple, classic approach to education. Many of the items included in our lesson plans are from time-tested traditional sources. Some books, like our readers have been used in Catholic Schools since the early 1900s. Others are recent publications published with very sound, traditional Catholic doctrine and modest illustrations, all with no infections of modernism or other heresies. We are excited to share these wonderful books with you and your students. We truly hope that you will enjoy teaching with us!

Our school year is based on 36 weeks.

These items are for sale in our store, which you can find at www.stjeromelibrary.org

Books Highly Recommended for Family Daily/Weekly Use with our Curriculum

We highly recommend Catholic families say each day their morning prayers, evening prayers, Angelus (or Regina Caeli during Eastertide), and Family Rosary. Making Spiritual Communions is greatly encouraged during these difficult times of ours, and you can make frequent visits to the cemetery to pray for the Holy Souls in Purgatory.

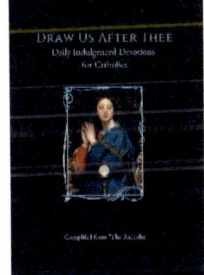

In aiding the family with young children, we highly recommend these incredible books to boost the spiritual life:

Draw Us after Thee: Daily Indulgenced Devotions for Catholics which has a different daily prayer and picture for every day of the year to enchance morning prayers. Catholics reap the benefits of never being in danger of a stale prayer life while learning about the different feasts of the Church and incredible indulgences She offers to us. Indulgences can be given to the Holy Souls in Purgatory as well!

Pictorial Lives of the Saints, which has wonderful short stories & reflections of the saints' lives for daily meditation. Great for inspiring questions and "teaching moments". Stories are fairly short as to keep children's attention.

The Pictorial Rosary is a great aid for meditation during the Family Rosary, as well as including the excellent prayers to Our Lady of Sorrows which adds an excellent addition to family night prayers.

Feeding God's People

Providence Pastures Co. is a nonprofit formed by us, exclusively for advancing the Kingship of Christ and helping Our Lady and St. Joseph harbor and advance the family and domestic Church. We have come to see ourselves as stewards of creation and hope to share the undeniable goodness and health benefits of pasture-raised, nutrient-dense food. In these trying times, we see our work as an apostolate from Our Blessed Mother to feed Her children by providing affordable, healthy foods, such as organic grass-fed and finished, pasture-raised beef, chicken, pork, maple syrup, wheat products, produce, and more. Visit our certified organic farm's website at www.pasturesofprovidence.com Contact us through the website if you are interested in food being shipped to you. May God be with you!

Grade Seven

Grammar – This year continues the use of the old Catholic *Voyages in English* series from the 1950s with our updated and beautiful *St. Jerome Grammar* series. The *St. Jerome Grammar 7* text will give your child the foundation necessary for excellent grammar skills. *St. Jerome Grammar 7 Teacher's Text Manual* will give the teacher instructions for teaching from the book, as well as the answers to the exercises within the text. The *St. Jerome Grammar 7 Workbook* is filled with fun and edifying color pictures to drive home what your student has learned from the text. The *St. Jerome Grammar 7 Workbook Answer Key* will help immensely in speeding the process of grading with handy side-by-side answers to match the workbooks. A grammar notebook can be used for assigning writing assignments as needed.

Logic – This year continues an incredible series which teaches the young Catholic an indispensable foundation of all definition and correct reasoning. This year's book is *Introduction to Correct Reasoning*. The logic books build the child's ability to communicate ideas, thoughts, and understanding accurately. Before beginning classes, parents should read "To the Student" on p. iii-iv.

Music – This grade continues the fun and secular series of *Doctor Mozart's Music Theory. Doctor Mozart Music Theory Workbook 1B* continues to give your child a strong musical foundation. By the end of the three books that are used throughout middle school, your student will have learned much which will serve them in the future. Also, we would highly recommend you introduce the student to some classical forms of music, such as Gregorian Chant, Masses, traditional Catholic songs, etc. Perhaps buy your student a new inexpensive instrument and see if they can try to learn to play it. Have fun!

History – This year continues with the classical Catholic history series *Catholic Voyages in History* which has been used for decades with Catholic schools, even to present day. *The Growth of Our Nation* set for this year includes the textbook, workbook, and answer key. This lesson plan book includes the quarterly exams used as well for the course. The workbook will be used with the textbook in finding answers for weekly assignments. Quarterly exams should be given. the parent/teacher may decide if they allow the student open-book exams or not, depending on what he/she believes to be the best for their student(s).

Reading – *St. Jerome School Reader 7* text is an incredible, classic Catholic reader that has been used for over a hundred years with students! The historical content helps children learn about times long past, including the beautiful speech that was used. We have found that often it helps if you alternate between reading lessons with your student, and then having him or her read the next one on their own. This gives good oral reading practice. Other literature books include *Flame of White, The Gauntlet,* and *St. John Bosco Stories*. These are all incredible works, difficult to put down, which also teach about history (including St. Pope Pius X and St. John Bosco). We recommend assigning book reports (located in the back for copying) after reading the books. A discussion of the books between teacher and student should also be present.

Religion - *Living My Religion Grade 7* is from the 1940s' imprimatured *Living My Religion* series which teaches catechism in a fun and traditional way. The text is written in an easy-to-read format so that the child feels invited and excited to practice reading with the simple text. *Bible History* will also be used to briefly go over our history, but not in a very intense way, simply for reading enjoyment and historical knowledge. *The World is His Parish: The Story of Pope Pius XII* is also included. It is a graphic novel relating the life of Pope Pius XII. It is simply wonderful for children to become more familiar with this pope of recent times and the crosses he carried. May he rest in peace.

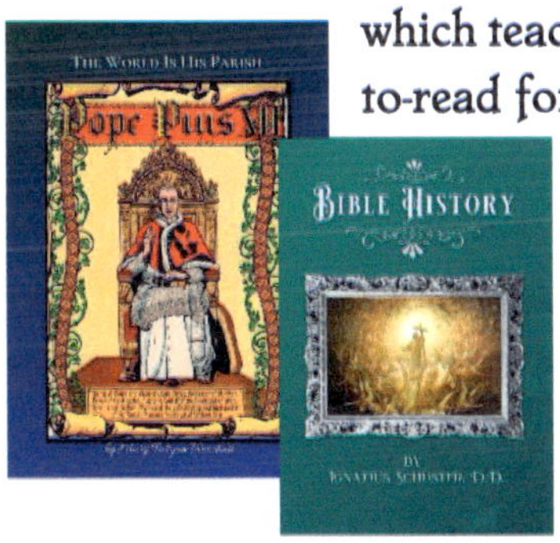

Math – This year's text will be *Saxon Math 8/7*. We highly recommend you also purchase *Saxon Math 8/7 Solutions Manual* to help with fast grading. If you trust your student, it may prove beneficial to have them grade their own math after they have done it to learn what they have done wrong. Teachers, of course, grade tests so they can gauge what the student has been learning well. This works well especially in large, busy families where a mother is trying to grade many children's lessons each day. It can be overwhelming! *Saxon Math 87 Tests & Worksheets* should also be purchased as the tests are in it, as well as the activities and math drills. We will only be doing one of each math drill. Teachers may assign more if she sees there is a great need for the student to work more on a particular skill.

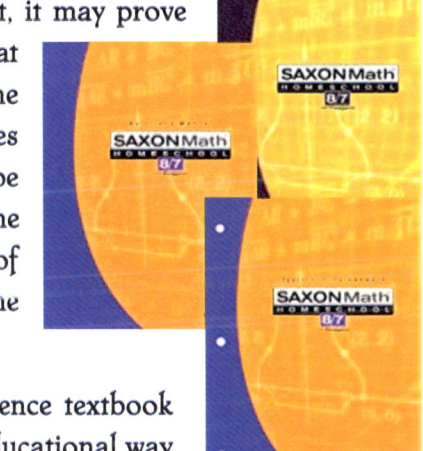

Science – *Science in God's World 7* is a classic and colorful science textbook which reflects the Catholic faith. It presents science in a simple, educational way with questions and basic facts, as well as providing opportunities to discuss the subjects with the teacher and offering optional experiments. We hope you will enjoy this series as we at St. Jerome Library Press have updated many of the pictures to include modern-day photos so that students will have excellent, solid scientific education along with the beautiful Catholic Faith infused throughout. The *Science in God's World 7 Workbook* will offer a splendid review of the concepts learned throughout the book, including a little fun humor to make learning a bit more fun. The *Science in God's World 7 Answer Key* is necessary for grading everything in this science course.

Spelling – This year's spelling continues with *Spelling Forest Grade 7*. This speller is filled with beautiful forest-themed pages, including many Catholic exercises, which make learning vocabulary, spelling, and a bit of handwriting practice one of our students' favorite activities. The words include Catholic terminology, along with words compiled from grade-appropriate standards used in national spelling bees and the like. If the teacher does not already own it, *St. Jerome Catholic Spellers Answer Key* will be essential for grading the "Fill in the Blank" and "Synonyms & Antonyms" sections of the workbook. A Spelling Notebook will be used to write the words for tests or as practice for those words that were done incorrectly on the pretest.

Summer Reading – For the summer, we would like to students to keep up their reading habits somewhat. The Summer Reading List for Grade 7 are the Windeatt books: *The Little Flower, The Cure of Ars, Saint Hyacinth of Poland,* and *Saint Louis de Montfort.* The book report form is in the back of this book.

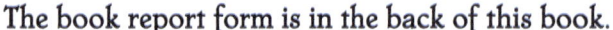

Student will also need:

Compass (drawing circles)

Folder for Completed Papers

Folder for Origami Papers

Graph Paper

Pencils

Pens

Protractor

Ruler w/cm & in

Scientific Calculator

Scissors

Notebooks for Grammar, Math, Science, and Spelling

In the lesson plan, * means refer to Comments section for the week

The Report Card is in the back for easy record keeping.

Sample

Spaces below the assignments are for grades, comments, time spent, etc.

	Kindergarten Lesson Plans		
Subject	Monday	Tuesday	Wednesday
Hand-writing & Phonics	-HK: Sing the ABC Song with student while on p. ix & count #'s, then p. xi-xiv	-HK: ABC Song with p. x, then p. 1-3 -ABC: Read p. 2-9	-HK: Review ABC's with student daily until understood, then p. 4-6 -ABC: Review p. 4-9
	N/A	95%	30min, 98%
Hand-writing & Phonics	-HK: p. 13-15 -ABC: p. 11-17	-HK: p. 16-18 -ABC: Review p. 11-17	-HK: p. 19-21 -ABC: Review p. 11-17
	100%, hard worker!	87%, rushed and distracted	92%

Book Abbreviations for Grade 7 Lesson Plans

Bible History = BH

Doctor Mozart 1B Music Theory = DM1B

Flame of White = FW

The Gauntlet = G

The Growth of Our Nation Text = GON

The Growth of Our Nation Workbook = GONWB

Introduction to Correct Reasoning = ICR

Living My Religion Grade 7 = LMR7

Saxon Math 8/7 Tests & Worksheets = SMTW7

Saxon Math 8/7 Text = SM7

Science in God's World 7 = SGW7

Science in God's World 7 Workbook = SGW7WB

Spelling Forest Grade 7 = SF

St. Jerome Grammar 7 Text = SJG7

St. Jerome Grammar 7 Workbook = SJG7WB

St. Jerome School Reader 7 = SJSR7

St. John Bosco Stories = SJBS

The World is His Parish = WHP

Week 1

Subject	Monday	Tuesday	Wednesday
Religion	-BH: p. 1-8, Student will read and stop at the end of a chapter, but does not need to answer questions, just understand the information.		-LMR7: p. 1-8 (Teacher & student may alternatively read to each other. Teacher orally asks test questions at the end of chapters.)
Logic & Spelling	-ICR: Read & discuss p. iii-iv & remove answer key from back -SF: p. 3-6, Student reads words aloud to teacher for correct*	-SF: p. 7-8	-ICR: Introduce p. 1, 3-9
Grammar	-SJG7: p. 213-222 Stop at "4. Case" (Reading can be done any time during the week.) It is recommended that teacher reads*	-SJG7WB: p. 5	-SJG7WB: p. 6
Reading	-SJSR7: p. 11-21 (Each day, one lesson to be orally read by teacher to student, and another by student to teacher.)*	-SJSR7: p. 20-27	
History		-GONWB: P. 1-4 (skip Section B, #6-10 on p. 1) complete with textbook	-GON: Read p. 1-4 -GONWB: p. 5
Math	-SM7: L. 1, student reads lessons to himself, then does Lesson Practice, and evens (or odds) only Mixed Practice in MN	-SM7: L. 2 -SMTW7: Facts Practice Test A (these may be done more than once if teacher wishes)	-SM7: L. 3
Science			
Music Theory			-DM1B: p. 2-3

Week 1

Subject	Thursday	Friday	Comments
Religion		-WHP: Read p. 1-9	
Logic & Spelling	-SF: Administer pre-test. Student writes words in Spelling notebook 3x each that are wrong.	-SF: Take Post-test for grade.	*pronunciation, then writes words as neatly as possible
Grammar	-SJG7WB: p. 7	-SJG7WB: p. 8	*to student & does some of the exercises in the book to gauge understanding. Workbooks assignments are done on their own.
Reading			*This gives the student both the good example of storytelling and the chance to practice it himself.
History			
Math	SM7: L. 4	-SM7: L. 5	
Science	-SGW7: Read p. 5-20	-SGW7WB: p. 3 -Questions throughout the textbook may be done as an optional review.	
Music Theory			

Week 2

Subject	Monday	Tuesday	Wednesday
Religion	-BH: p. 8-13		-LMR7: p. 8-18
Logic & Spelling	-ICR: Inroduce p. 10-11 -SF: p. 9-12, Lesson 2	-SF: p. 13-14	-ICR: Review p. 12
Grammar	-SJG7: p. 1-27, 222-224 (Stop at "Nominative in Apposition")*	-SJG7WB: p. 9	-SJG7WB: p. 10
Reading	-SJSR7: p. 28-36	-SJSR7: p. 37-46	
History		-GON: Read p. 6-18 -GONWB: p. 6-7	-GON: Read p. 19-24 -GONWB: p. 8-9
Math	-SM7: L. 6	-SM7: L. 7	-SM7: L. 8 -SMTW7: FPT B
Science			
Music Theory			-DM1B: p. 4

Subject	Thursday	Friday	Comments
Religion		-WHP: Read p. 10-18	
Logic & Spelling	-SF: Administer pre-test. Student writes words in Spelling notebook 3x each that are wrong.	-SF: Take Post-test for grade.	
Grammar	-SJG7WB: p. 11	-SJG7WB: p. 12	*Teacher will assign writing assignments from SJG7 according to the student's needs, to be written in his Grammar notebook.
Reading			
History			
Math	-SM7: L. 9	-SM7: L. 10	
Science	-SGW7: Read p. 20-27	-SGW7WB: p. 4	
Music Theory			

Week 3

Subject	Monday	Tuesday	Wednesday
Religion	-BH: p. 13-17		-LMR7: p. 19-23
Logic & Spelling	-ICR: Introduce p. 2, 13-17 -SF: p. 15-18, Lesson 3	-SF: p. 19-20	-ICR: p. 18-19
Grammar	-SJG7: p. 28-55 (fix immodest pictures throughout the book), p. 224-230 (Stop at "Objective Case")	-SJG7WB: p. 13 (p. 14 for extra credit, if desired)	-SJG7WB: p. 15
Reading	-SJSR7: p. 47-53	-SJSR7: p. 54-63	
History		-GON: Read p. 24-31 -GONWB: p. 10	-GON: Read p. 32-36 -GONWB: p. 11-12
Math	-SMTW7: Test 1 (Show all work on loose leaf paper or notebook)	-SM7: Investigation 1* -SMTW7: Activity Sheets 1-6	-SM7: L. 11 -SMTW7: FPT C
Science			
Music Theory			-DM1B: p. 5

Week 3

Subject	Thursday	Friday	Comments
Religion		-WHP: Read p. 19-27	
Logic & Spelling	-SF: Administer pre-test. Student writes words in Spelling notebook 3x each that are wrong.	-SF: Take Post-test for grade.	
Grammar	-SJG7WB: p. 16	-SJG7WB: p. 17	
Reading			
History			
Math	-SM7: L. 12	-SM7: L. 13	*Sometimes investigations can be complicated and confusing. They can be counted as extra credit only if the teacher wishes.
Science	-SGW7: Read p. 27-35, Do experiments as time allows at teacher's discretion throughout the year	-SGW7WB: p. 5	
Music Theory			

Week 4

Subject	Monday	Tuesday	Wednesday
Religion	-BH: p. 18-25		-LMR7: p. 23-30
Logic & Spelling	-ICR: p. 20-22 -SF: p. 21-24, Lesson 4	-SF: p. 25-26	-ICR: Introduce p. 23-27
Grammar	-SJG7: p. 56-85, 230-233	-SJG7WB: p. 18	-SJG7WB: p. 19
Reading	-SJSR7: p. 64-70	-SJSR7: p. 71-81	
History		-GON: Read p. 36-44 -GONWB: p. 13-14	-GON: Read p. 45-52 -GONWB: p. 15-17
Math	-SM7: L. 14	-SM7: L. 15	-SMTW7: Test 2
Science			
Music Theory			-DM1B: p. 6

Week 4

Subject	Thursday	Friday	Comments
Religion		-WHP: Read p. 28-35 (end!)	
Logic & Spelling	-SF: Administer pre-test. Student writes words in Spelling notebook 3x each that are wrong.	-SF: Take Post-test for grade.	
Grammar	-SJG7WB: p. 20	-SJG7WB: p. 21	
Reading			
History			
Math	-SM7: L. 16	-SM7: L. 17	
Science	-SGW7: Read p. 36-47	-SGW7WB: p. 6	
Music Theory			

Week 5

Subject	Monday	Tuesday	Wednesday
Religion	-BH: p. 25-29		-LMR7: p. 30-36
Logic & Spelling	-ICR: p. 28-33 -SF: p. 27-30, L. 5	-SF: p. 31-32	-ICR: p. 34-37
Grammar	-SJG7: p. 86-117, 234-238	-SJG7WB: p. 22	-SJG7WB: p. 23
Reading	-SJSR7: p. 82-89	-SJSR7: p. 90-98	
History		-GON: Read p. 53-65 -GONWB: p. 18-20	-GON: Read p. 65-76 -GONWB: p. 21-22
Math	-SM7: L. 18	-SM7: L. 19	-SM7: L. 20 -SMTW7: FPT D
Science			
Music Theory			-DM1B: p. 7

Week 5

Subject	Thursday	Friday	Comments
Religion		-BH: p. 30-34	
Logic & Spelling	-SF: Administer pre-test. Student writes words in Spelling notebook 3x each that are wrong.	-SF: Take Post-test for grade.	
Grammar	-SJG7WB: p. 24 (p. 25 for extra credit)	-SJG7WB: p. 26 (p. 27 extra credit)	
Reading			
History	-GON: p. 76-81 (optional extra credit only)		
Math	-SMTW7: Test 3	-SM7: Investigation 2	
Science	-SGW7: Read p. 51-58	-SGW7WB: p. 7	
Music Theory			

Week 6

Subject	Monday	Tuesday	Wednesday
Religion	-BH: p. 35-40		-LMR7: p. 37-43
Logic & Spelling	-ICR: Introduce p. 38-39 -SF: p. 33-36, L. 6	-SF: p. 37-38	-ICR: p. 40-43
Grammar	-SJG7: p. 239-249	-SJG7WB: p. 28	-SJG7WB: p. 29
Reading	-SJSR7: p. 99-106	-SJSR7: p. 107-113	
History		-GONWB: p. 23-25	-GON: Read p. 84-91 -GONWB: p. 26-27
Math	-SM7: L. 21	-SM7: L. 22	-SM7: L. 23 -SMTW7: FPT E
Science			
Music Theory			-DM1B: p. 8

Week 6

Subject	Thursday	Friday	Comments
Religion		-BH: p. 40-46	
Logic & Spelling	-SF: Administer pre-test. Student writes words in Spelling notebook 3x each that are wrong.	-SF: Take Post-test for grade.	
Grammar	-SJG7WB: p. 30	-SJG7WB: p. 31	
Reading			
History			
Math	-SM7: L. 24	-SM7: L. 25	
Science	-SGW7: Read p. 58-70	-SGW7WB: p. 8	
Music Theory			

Week 7

Subject	Monday	Tuesday	Wednesday
Religion	-BH: p. 47-52		-LMR7: p. 43-50
Logic & Spelling	-ICR: p. 44-48 -SF: p. 39-42, L. 7	-SF: p. 43-44	-ICR: p. 49-50
Grammar	-SJG7: p. 118-151, 250-255 (Stop at "Predicate Nominative")	-SJG7WB: p. 32	-SJG7WB: p. 33
Reading	-SJSR7: p. 114-122	-SJSR7: p. 123-129	
History		-GON: Read p. 91-98 -GONWB: p. 28	-GON: Read p. 99-106 -GONWB: p. 29-30
Math	-SMTW7: Test 4	-SM7: L. 26	-SM7: L. 27 -SMTW7: FPT F
Science			
Music Theory			-DM1B: p. 9

Week 7

Subject	Thursday	Friday	Comments
Religion		-BH: p. 53-58	
Logic & Spelling	-SF: Administer pre-test. Student writes words in Spelling notebook 3x each that are wrong.	-SF: Take Post-test for grade.	
Grammar	-SJG7WB: p. 34	-SJG7WB: p. 35	
Reading			
History			
Math	-SM7: L. 28	-SM7: L. 29	
Science	-SGW7: Read p. 70-80	-SGW7WB: p. 9	
Music Theory			

Week 8

Subject	Monday	Tuesday	Wednesday
Religion	-BH: p. 58-64		-LMR7: p. 50-54
Logic & Spelling	-ICR: Introduce p. 51-55 -SF: p. 45-48, L. 8	-SF: p. 49-50	-ICR: p. 56-58
Grammar	-SJG7: p. 152-169, 255-259 (Stop at "Object of a Preposition")	-SJG7WB: p. 36	-SJG7WB: p. 37
Reading	-SJSR7: p. 130-136	-SJSR7: p. 137-144	
History		-GON: Read p. 106-113 -GONWB: p. 31-32	-GON: Read p. 114-120 -GONWB: p. 33-34
Math	-SM7: L. 30	-SMTW7: Test 5	-SM7: Investigation 3
Science			
Music Theory			-DM1B: p. 10

Week 8

Subject	Thursday	Friday	Comments
Religion		-BH: p. 65-70	
Logic & Spelling	-SF: Administer pre-test. Student writes words in Spelling notebook 3x each that are wrong.	-SF: Take Post-test for grade.	
Grammar	-SJG7WB: p. 38	-SJG7WB: p. 39	
Reading			
History			
Math	-SM7: L. 31	-SM7: L. 32	
Science	-SGW7: Read p. 80-92	-SGW7WB: p. 10	
Music Theory			

Week 9

Subject	Monday	Tuesday	Wednesday
Religion	-BH: p. 71-77		-LMR7: p. 55-64
Logic & Spelling	-ICR: p. 59-61		-ICR: p. 62-68
Grammar	-SJG7: p. 170-189 (explain modern changes), 259-264 (Stop at "5. Drill on Relative Pronouns")	-SJG7WB: p. 40 (p. 41 for extra credit)	-SJG7WB: p. 42
Reading	-SJSR7: p. 145-154	-SJSR7: p. 155-161	
History		-GON: Read p. 120-126 -GONWB: p. 35-36	-GONWB: p. 38-39 -Study for First Quarter Exam
Math	-SM7: L. 33	-Review any needed math lessons	-SM7: L. 34 -SMTW7: FPT G
Science			
Music Theory			-DM1B: p. 11

Week 9

Subject	Thursday	Friday	Comments
Religion		-BH: p. 78-83	
Logic & Spelling			
Grammar	-SJG7WB: p. 43-44	-SJG7WB: p. 45	
Reading			
History	-First Quarter Exam (remove from 2 pages from here)		
Math	-SM7: L. 35	-SM1W7: Test 6	
Science	-SGW7: Study for First Quarter Exam	-First Quarter Exam (remove 8 pages from here)	
Music Theory			

First Quarter History Exam

The Growth of Our Nation

Grade 7

Name _____

True or False (30 points).

1. _____ Jackson was always in agreement with the Supreme Court and John Marshall.

2. _____ Jackson was the first president from the West.

3. _____ In the election of 1824, Jackson received more popular votes than any other candidate.

4. _____ Jackson was determined to destroy the Bank of the United States.

5. _____ Jackson's followers were happy that he was not elected president in 1824.

6. _____ Andrew Jackson can be best described as a hasty, stubborn, courageous aristocrat.

7. _____ John C. Calhoun wrote the South Carolina Exposition.

8. _____ Nullification means that a state has the right to declare that a federal law is null and void.

9. _____ Captain Gray discovered the Columbia River.

10. _____ The Rocky Mountains at the close of the Revolutionary War was the western boundary of the United States in 1783.

Fill in the Blanks (not all of the words will be used). (30 points)

California	Wisconsin	Tippecanoe
gigantic celery	abolitionists	Andrew Jackson
immigrants	Harpers Ferry	Fr. De Smet
underground railroad	Robert Hayne	hidden subway

1. _____ was called Old Hickory by his followers.

2. _____ opposed Daniel Webster in a famous debate.

3. _____ represented the U.S. government in its efforts to bring peace between the Indians and the white settlers in the Far West.

4. Cotton and rice were the only staple crops in the state of _____.

5. William Henry Harrison was the hero of the battle of _____.

6. Those who were opposed to slavery were called anti-slavery men or _____.

7. A system for freeing negro slaves was called the _____.

8. One of the provisions of the Compromise of 1850 was that _____ should be admitted as a free state.

9. German and Irish _____ who had known oppression in their native lands, favored the principals expressed in the free states.

10. Robert E. Lee was in charge of federal troops at _____.

Short Essay Questions. (40 points)

Essay answers are to be written in complete sentences. Each answer is worth four points. Think of the best possible answer before you write.

1. Why did the Texans dislike Mexican rule? Give at least two reasons.

2. Explain the Gadsden Purchase.

3. Before Oregon became a part of the United States, what other countries had overlapping claims to that territory? How was the dispute finally settled?

4. How did the missionaries help to develop the West? Name at least two of them in your answer.

5. What were some of the problems that forty-niners (49ers) and the Californians had to deal with during the gold rush?

6. Explain what a "dark horse means.

7. What was the Pony Express, and how was Buffalo Bill connected with it?

8. Explain what the Homestead Act was and what it encouraged.

9. Why was Fr. De Smet chosen by the United States government as its representative among the Indians?

10. Explain what "Remember the Alamo" means.

First Quarter Science Exam
Science in God's World 7
Grade 7

Name _____

Directions: on the blank line, write the letter preceding the word or expression that best completes the statement

_____ 1. The Creator of all science is
    a. God
    b. Aristotle
    c. Leonardo de Vinci
    d. Bob Smith

_____ 2. According to the scientific method, a theory is not accepted as a fact until
    a. it has been disproved by many experiments
    b. it has been proved correct by one experiment
    c. it has been proved correct by many experiments
    d. it has been disproved by one experiment

_____ 3. The Greek physician who studied medical records and kept careful records of his observations was
    a. Socrates
    b. Archimedes
    c. Pythagoras
    d. Hippocrates

_____ 4. The Greek scientist who reasoned that the amount of weight lost by a submerged object would be equal to the weight of the water that is displaced was
    a. Socrates
    b. Archimedes
    c. Pythagoras
    d. Hippocrates

_____ 5. The first scientist to suggest the theory that all the planets, including the earth, are moving around the sun was the Polish astronomer
    a. Gregor Mendel
    b. Nicholas Copernicus
    c. Leonardo da Vinci
    d. Galileo Galilei

_____ 6. The Italian astronomer Galileo Galilei was able to do most of his studies due primarily to the
    a. invention of the telescope
    b. invention of the gyroscope
    c. invention of the microscope
    d. exhaustive library research

_____ 7. Scientists are careful to arrange facts in an orderly way
    a. to impress other scientists
    b. to keep the information organized
    c. in order to see a connection among them
    d. to prepare for publication

_____ 8. The process of drawing conclusions from information is called
    a. experimentation
    b. guessing
    c. reasoning
    d. publishing results

_____ 9. An explanation or idea based on observation and reasoning is called
    a. a theory
    b. a fact
    c. an observation
    d. a conclusion

_____ 10. Something seen and noted is
    a. a theory
    b. an observation
    c. a fact
    d. a hypothesis

_____ 11. Knowledge gained by means of careful observation and experimentation is called
    a. experience
    b. education
    c. exercises
    d. learning

_____ 12. A decision or answer to a question reached by reasoning is called
    a. a fact
    b. a theory
    c. a result
    d. a conclusion

_____ 13. Knowledge of the facts about God's world arranged in an orderly way is called
    a. art
    b. superstition
    c. science
    d. technology

_____ 14. A scientist who studies the stars and other heavenly bodies
    a. meteorologist
    b. astronomer
    c. astrologer
    d. geologist

_____ 15. A statement that describes certain conditions that always produce the same results is known as
    a. a scientific principle
    b. a principle of nature
    c. a law of nature
    d. a scientific theory

_____ 16. If the results of repeated experimentation do not agree with a scientific theory
    a. the theory is close to becoming a law of nature
    b. the theory does not need to be changed
    c. the theory is scientifically sound
    d. the theory must be changed

_____ 17. John Dalton, an English schoolmaster and scientist, was interested in the causes and effects of
    a. color-blindness
    b. diabetes
    c. near-sightedness
    d. double-vision

_____ 18. The smallest particle of an element is called
    a. a molecule
    b. an atom
    c. a compound
    d. an element

_____ 19. Materials that cannot be broken down into simpler substances are
    a. compounds
    b. elements
    c. molecules
    d. atoms

_____ 20. Materials that can be broken down into simpler substances are
   a. molecules
   b. elements
   c. compounds
   d. atoms

_____ 21. Dalton believed that an atom
   a. could not be split
   b. could be split
   c. could be destroyed
   d. could not combine with other atoms

_____ 22. Rayon, dacron (polyester), and nylon are
   a. elements
   b. compounds
   c. natural materials
   d. man-made materials

_____ 23. The science that treats of the make-up of the molecules of substances and of the changes in substances is known as
   a. physics
   b. astronomy
   c. chemistry
   d. biology

_____ 24. Rays that go through materials that an ordinary light ray cannot go through are
   a. cosmic rays
   b. x-rays
   c. gamma rays
   d. ultraviolet rays

_____ 25. Creatures that have backbones are known as
   a. vertebrates
   b. invertebrates
   c. mammals
   d. chordates

_____ 26. Warm-blooded animals that have hair and whose young are born alive are classified as
   a. ungulates
   b. reptiles
   c. mammals
   d. birds

_____ 27. The only creature that gets sunburned
   a. man
   b. birds
   c. apes
   d. horses

_____ 28. An example of an invertebrate
   a. amphibian
   b. birds
   c. fish
   d. grasshoppers

_____ 29. A person who eats vegetables but no meat is
   a. carnivorous
   b. herbivorous
   c. vegetarian
   d. insectivorous

_____ 30. Scientists separate the parts of the human body into
   a. four systems
   b. five systems
   c. seven systems
   d. nine systems

_____ 31. The number of bones in the human body is about
        a. 106   b. 206   c. 306   d. 506

_____ 32. The system of bones which form the framework of the body is called
        a. the respiratory system   c. the excretory system
        b. the skeleton system   d. the digestive system

_____ 33. The purpose of the skeleton system is to
        a. support the rest of the body
        b. protect the delicate parts of the body
        c. provide a system of levers by which the body moves
        d. all of the above

_____ 34. A firm, elastic, almost clear, flexible material forming parts of the skeleton system
        a. marrow   c. cartilage
        b. joints   d. platelets

_____ 35. Red blood cells and most of the white blood cells of the body are produced in the
        a. yellow marrow cavity   c. the red and yellow cavities
        b. red marrow cavity   d. the white marrow cavity

_____ 36. Platelets, found in red bone marrow, help blood to
        a. thin   c. circulate
        b. clot   d. resist infection

_____ 37. Muscles which work only when you make them do so are called
        a. simple muscles   c. voluntary muscles
        b. involuntary muscles   d. complex muscles

_____ 38. Under a microscope, heart muscle looks like
        a. simple muscles   c. voluntary muscles
        b. involuntary muscles   d. complex muscles

_____ 39. Voluntary muscle cells are
        a. made up of long string-like cells called muscle fibers
        b. shaped like separate spindle-shaped cells that come to a point

_____ 40. The large muscles in the front part of the upper arm are the
        a. capillaries   c. tendons
        b. triceps   d. biceps

_____ 41. The tough, strong band or cord that joins a muscle to a bone is called the
        a. biceps   c. tendons
        b. triceps   d. capillaries

(over)

_____ 42. An injury caused by too much effort or by stretching is
      a. a puncture   c. an abrasion
      b. a fracture   d. a strain

_____ 43. The proper sequence of the main parts of the digestive system is
      a. mouth, esophagus, stomach, large intestine, small intestine
      b. mouth, esophagus, stomach, small intestine, large intestine
      c. mouth, esophagus, small intestine, stomach, large intestine
      d. mouth, stomach, esophagus, small intestine, large intestine

_____ 44. Saliva begins the digestion of
      a. protein foods   b. starchy foods   c. fatty foods

_____ 45. Dr. William Beaumont discovered that the usual stomach temperature is
      a. 98.5°F   b. 100°   c. 102°F   d. 105°F

_____ 46. Teeth
      a. are not really bones
      b. have roots and crowns
      c. require calcium and vitamin D for normal growth
      d. all of the above

_____ 47. The esophagus
      a. digests starchy foods
      b. digests protein foods
      c. force food towards the stomach by means of involuntary muscles
      d. force food towards the stomach by means of voluntary muscles

_____ 48. Digested food in the little intestine is absorbed into the blood stream by means of
      a. lipase   b. rennin   c. pepsin   d. villi

_____ 49. Saliva changes starch into a special kind of sugar called
      a. sucrose   b. maltose   c. glucose   d. fructose

_____ 50. The liver releases a digestive juice called
      a. bile   b. saliva   c. gastric juice   d. chyme

Grade 7 Second Quarter

Week 10

Subject	Monday	Tuesday	Wednesday
Religion	-BH: p. 83-90		-LMR7: p. 65-72
Logic & Spelling	-ICR: p. 69 -SF: p. 51-54, L. 9	-SF: p. 55-56	-ICR: p. 69, compose statements with a 3rd choice of predicate on loose leaf paper
Grammar	-SJG7: p. 190-210 (explain modern changes), 264-265 (Stop at "6. Agreement with Distributive and Indefinite Pronouns")	-SJG7WB: p. 46	-SJG7WB: p. 47
Reading	-SJSR7: p. 162-172	-SJSR7: p. 173-183	
History		-GON: Read p. 127-134 -GONWB: p. 37	-GON: Read p. 134-140 -GONWB: p. 38-39
Math	-SM7: L. 36	-SM7: L. 37	-SM7: L. 38
Science			
Music Theory			-DMIB: p. 12

Week 10

Subject	Thursday	Friday	Comments
Religion		-BH: p. 90-95	
Logic & Spelling	-SF: Administer pre-test. Student writes words in Spelling notebook 3x each that are wrong.	-SF: Take Post-test for grade.	
Grammar	-SJG7WB: p. 48	-SJG7WB: p. 49	
Reading			
History	-GONWB: p. 40		
Math	-SM7: L. 39	-SM7: L. 40	
Science	-SGW7: Read p. 92-99	-SGW7WB: p. 11	
Music Theory			

Week 11

Subject	Monday	Tuesday	Wednesday
Religion	-BH: p. 95-102		-LMR7: p. 73-79
Logic & Spelling	-ICR: Introduce p. 70-74 -SF: p. 57-60, L. 10	-SF: p. 61-62	-ICR: p. 75-76
Grammar	-SJG7: p. 265-268	-SJG7WB: p. 50-51 (Student may skip answering syntax question on line if teacher is okay with that, p. 52 extra credit)	-SJG7WB: p. 53
Reading	-SJSR7: p. 184-189	-SJSR7: p. 190-195	
History		-GON: Read p. 140-150 -GONWB: p. 41-42	-GON: Read p. 150-158 -GONWB: p. 43-44
Math	-SMTW7: Test 7	-SM7: Investigation 4	-SM7: L. 41 -SMTW7: FPT H
Science			
Music Theory			-DM1B: p. 13

Week 11

Subject	Thursday	Friday	Comments
Religion		-BH: p. 103-109	
Logic & Spelling	-SF: Administer pre-test. Student writes words in Spelling notebook 3x each that are wrong.	-SF: Take Post-test for grade.	
Grammar	-SJG7WB: p. 54	-SJG7WB: p. 55 (p. 56 extra credit)	
Reading			
History	-GONWB: p. 45		
Math	-SM7: L. 42	-SM7: L. 43 -SMTW7: FPT I	
Science	-SGW7: Read p. 99-104	-SGW7WB: p. 12	
Music Theory			

Subject	Monday	Tuesday	Wednesday
Religion	-BH: p. 109-116		-LMR7: p. 79-90
Logic & Spelling	-ICR: Introduce p. 77-82 -SF: p. 63-66, L. 11	-SF: p. 67-68	-ICR: p. 83-89
Grammar	-SJG7: p. 269-276 (Stop at "Comparison of Adjectives")	-SJG7WB: p. 57	-SJG7WB: p. 58
Reading	-SJSR7: p. 196-204	-SJSR7: p. 205-213	
History		-GON: Read p. 159-165 -GONWB: p. 46-47	-GON: Read p. 165-173 -GONWB: p. 48
Math	-SM7: L. 44	-SM7: L. 45	-SMTW7: Test 8
Science			
Music Theory			-DM1B: p. 14

Week 12

Week 12

Subject	Thursday	Friday	Comments
Religion		-BH: p. 116-123	
Logic & Spelling	-SF: Administer pre-test. Student writes words in Spelling notebook 3x each that are wrong.	-SF: Take Post-test for grade.	
Grammar	-SJG7WB: p. 59	-SJG7WB: p. 60	
Reading			
History	-GON: Read p. 173-179 -GONWB: p. 49		
Math	-SM7: L. 46	-SM7: L. 47	
Science	-SGW7: Read p. 109-119	-SGW7WB: p. 13	
Music Theory			

Week 13

Subject	Monday	Tuesday	Wednesday
Religion	-BH: p. 123-128		-LMR7: p. 91-98
Logic & Spelling	-ICR: p. 90-95 -SF: p. 69-72, L. 12	-SF: p. 73-74	-ICR: p. 96-100
Grammar	-SJG7: p. 276-283 (Stop at "5. Words Used as Nouns and Adjectives)	-SJG7WB: p. 61	-SJG7WB: p. 62
Reading	-SJSR7: p. 215-220	-SJSR7: p. 221-225	
History		-GONWB: p. 50-51	-GON: p. 182-183 Unit Tests (optional extra credit)
Math	-SM7: L. 48	-SM7: L. 49	-SM7: L. 50
Science			
Music Theory			-DM1B: p. 15

Week 13

Subject	Thursday	Friday	Comments
Religion		-BH: p. 129-135	
Logic & Spelling	-SF: Administer pre-test. Student writes words in Spelling notebook 3x each that are wrong.	-SF: Take Post-test for grade.	
Grammar	-SJG7WB: p. 63	-SJG7WB: p. 64	
Reading			
History	-GON: Read p. 186-196 -GONWB: p. 52-53		
Math	-SMTW7: Test 9	-SM7: Investigation 5	
Science	-SGW7: Read p. 119-126	-SGW7WB: p. 14	
Music Theory			

Week 14

Subject	Monday	Tuesday	Wednesday
Religion	-BH: p. 136-141		-LMR7: p. 98-108
Logic & Spelling	-ICR: Introduce & do p. 101-105 -SF: p. 75-78, L. 13	-SF: p. 79-80	-ICR: Introduce & do p. 106-108
Grammar	-SJG7: p. 283-292 (Stop at "Copulative Verbs")	-SJG7WB: p. 65 (p. 66 extra credit)	-SJG7WB: p. 67
Reading	-SJSR7: p. 226-233	-SJSR7: p. 234-240 (end!)	
History		-GON: Read p. 196-201 -GONWB: p. 54	-GON: Read p. 201-206 -GONWB: p. 55
Math	-SM7: L. 51 -SMTW7: FPT J	-SM7: L. 52	-SM7: L. 53 -SMTW7: FPT K
Science			
Music Theory			-DM1B: p. 16

Week 14

Subject	Thursday	Friday	Comments
Religion		-BH: p. 141-147	
Logic & Spelling	-SF: Administer pre-test. Student writes words in Spelling notebook 3x each that are wrong.	-SF: Take Post-test for grade.	
Grammar	-SJG7WB: p. 68	-SJG7WB: p. 69	
Reading	-G: p. 11-23		
History	-GON: Read p. 206-212 -GONWB: p. 56-57		
Math	-SM7: L. 54	-SM7: L. 55	
Science	-SGW7: Read p. 126-142	-SGW7WB: p. 15	
Music Theory			

Week 15

Subject	Monday	Tuesday	Wednesday
Religion	-BH: p. 147-153		-LMR7: p. 109-114
Logic & Spelling	-ICR: p. 109-110 -SF: p. 81-84, L. 14	-SF: p. 85-86	-ICR: p. 111-112
Grammar	-SJG7: p. 292-295 (Stop at "Attributes or Qualities of a Verb")	-SJG7WB: p. 70	-SJG7WB: p. 71
Reading	-G: p. 24-35	-G: p. 36-42	
History		-GON: Read p. 213-227 -GONWB: p. 58-59	-GON: Read p. 227-236 -GONWB: p. 60-61
Math	-SMTW7: Test 10	-SM7: L. 56	-SM7: L. 57
Science			
Music Theory			-DMIB: p. 17

Week 15

Subject	Thursday	Friday	Comments
Religion		-BH: p. 153-158	
Logic & Spelling	-SF: Administer pre-test. Student writes words in Spelling notebook 3x each that are wrong.	-SF: Take Post-test for grade.	
Grammar	-SJG7WB: p. 72	-SJG7WB: p. 73	
Reading	-G: p. 43-51		
History	-GON: Read p. 237-248 -GONWB: p. 62		
Math	-SM7: L. 58	-SM7: L. 59 -SMTW7: FPT L	
Science	-SGW7: Read p. 143-158	-SGW7WB: p. 16	
Music Theory			

Week 16

Subject	Monday	Tuesday	Wednesday
Religion	-BH: p. 159-165		-LMR7: p. 114-121
Logic & Spelling	-ICR: p. 113-114 -SF: p. 87-90, L. 15	-SF: p. 91-92	-ICR: p. 115-116
Grammar	-SJG7: p. 295-299	-SJG7WB: p. 74	-SJG7WB: p. 75
Reading	-G: p. 52-64	-G: p. 65-81	
History		-GON: Read p. 248-252 -GONWB: p. 63-64	-GON: Read p. 253-257 -GONWB: p. 65
Math	-SM7: L. 60	-SMTW7: Test 11	-SM7: Investigation 6
Science			
Music Theory			-DM1B: p. 18

Week 16

Subject	Thursday	Friday	Comments
Religion		-BH: p. 165-172	
Logic & Spelling	-SF: Administer pre-test. Student writes words in Spelling notebook 3x each that are wrong.	-SF: Take Post-test for grade.	
Grammar	-SJG7WB: p. 76	-SJG7WB: p. 77	
Reading	-G: p. 82-91		
History			
Math	-SM7: L. 61	-SM7: L. 62	
Science	-SGW7: Read p. 158-163	-SGW7WB: p. 17	
Music Theory			

Week 17

Subject	Monday	Tuesday	Wednesday
Religion	-BH: p. 172-179		-LMR7: p. 122-126
Logic & Spelling	-ICR: p. 117 -SF: p. 93-96, L. 16	-SF: p. 97-98	-ICR: p. 118-119
Grammar	-SJG7: 300-313 (Stop at "Phrases and Parenthetical Expressions")	-SJG7WB: p. 78 (p. 79 extra credit)	-SJG7WB: p. 80
Reading	-G: p. 92-105	-G: p. 106-122	
History		-GON: Read p. 258-266 -GONWB: p. 66	-GON: Read p. 266-274 -GONWB: p. 67
Math	-SM7: L. 63	-SM7: L. 64	-SM7: L. 65
Science			
Music Theory			-DM1B: p. 19

Week 17

Subject	Thursday	Friday	Comments
Religion		-BH: p. 180-185	
Logic & Spelling	-SF: Administer pre-test. Student writes words in Spelling notebook 3x each that are wrong.	-SF: Take Post-test for grade.	
Grammar	-SJG7WB: p. 81	-SJG7WB: p. 82	
Reading	-G: p. 123-134		
History	-GONWB: p. 68-70		
Math	-SMTW7: Test 12	-SM7: L. 66 -SMTW7: FPT M	
Science	-SGW7: Read p. 163-173	-SGW7WB: p. 18	
Music Theory			

Week 18

Subject	Monday	Tuesday	Wednesday
Religion	-BH: p. 186-191		
Logic & Spelling	-ICR: p. 120-124		-Review p. 120-124
Grammar	-SJG7: 313-315 (Stop at "Compound Subjects Connected by 'Each' and 'Every'")	-SJG7WB: p. 83	-SJG7WB: p. 84
Reading	-G: p. 135-149	-G: p. 150-161	
History		-GON: p. 275-278 Unit Tests (optional extra credit)	-GON: Study for Second Quarter Exam (Ch. 9-14)
Math	-SM7: L. 67	-SM7: L. 68	-SM7: L. 69
Science			
Music Theory			-DM1B: p. 20

Week 18

Subject	Thursday	Friday	Comments
Religion		-BH: p. 192-199	
Logic & Spelling			
Grammar	-SJG7WB: p. 85		
Reading	-G: p. 162-175		
History	-Second Quarter Exam (Remove 2 pages from here)		
Math			
Science	Study for Second Quarter Exam (p. 92-173)	-Second Quarter Exam (remove 8 pages from here)	
Music Theory			

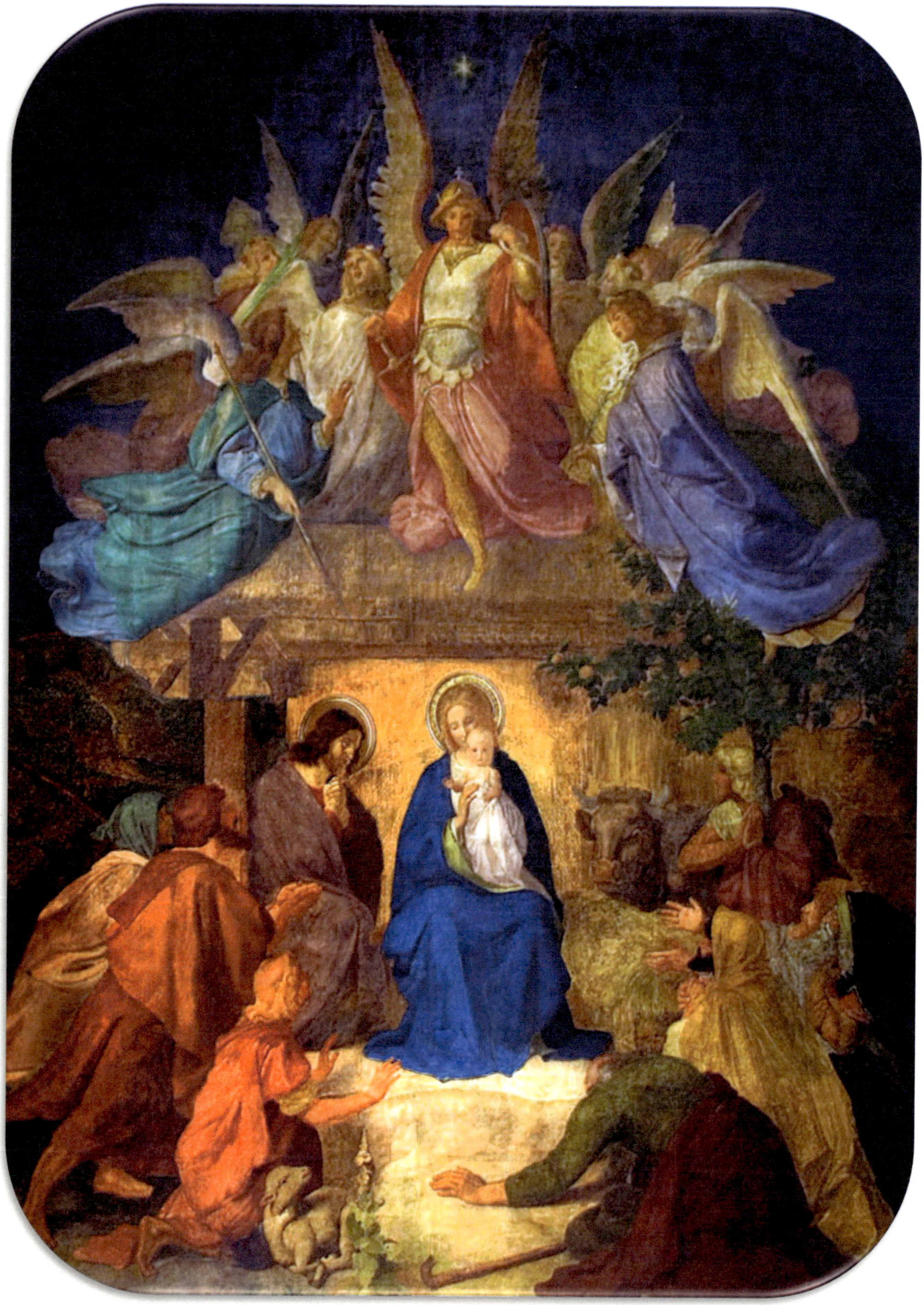

Second Quarter History Exam

The Growth of Our Nation

Grade 7

Name _____

True or False (30 points)

1. _____ A system for freeing Negro slaves was called the Liberator.

2. _____ Impeachment means that an office of the government is guilty of treason, bribery, or other crimes and misdemeanors.

3. _____ The compromise of 1850 is often called the Missouri Compromise.

4. _____ General Ulysses S. Grant led the Union troops in the famous march to the sea.

5. _____ The Maine was a United States warship sent to a harbor to protect American citizens there.

6. _____ The Rough Riders were a group of American volunteers under the command of Lieutenant Colonel Theodore Roosevelt.

7. _____ The Webster-Ashburton Treaty of 1842 fixed the boundaries between Alaska and Maine.

8. _____ George W. Goethals supervised the construction of the Panama Canal.

9. _____ The Big Stick Policy placed emphasis on preparedness or ability of the United States to protect itself.

10. _____ The region devoted to the raising of cotton is called the white belt.

11. _____ "Jacksonian Democracy" meant that the government should be carried on by the people.

12. _____ The Louisiana Purchase of 1803 doubled the size of the United States with land purchased from England.

13. _____ The term "manifest destiny" was used by expansionists as a reason why the United States should own all lands from the Atlantic to the Pacific and from the Great Lakes to the Gulf of Mexico.

14. _____ Father De Smet worked with the United States government to arrange peace treaties with the Mexicans.

15. _____ Sam Houston was elected President of the Confederate States of America.

Fill in the Blanks (some will not be used) (30 points):

Civil War	Hawaii	McKinley
Hawaii	Perry	Nigeria
Alaska	William McKinley	Guam
United States	13th	18th
14th	Hungary	Abraham Lincoln
"dollar diplomacy"	England	hug train

1. As a result of the Spanish-American War, the United States gained possession of the Philippines, Puerto Rico, and _____.

2. The United States and _____ disagreed concerning the protection of the seals in the Bering Sea.

3. President _____ refused to purchase Cuba because he did not want to buy a revolution.

4. The newspaper king of New York was Joseph Pulitzer, a native of _____.

5. The Naval officer who opened Japanese ports to western trade was Commodore _____.

6. The Sandwich Islands, or _____ Islands, as they are now called, were important stepping stones between Oregon and China.

7. The United States purchased _____ from Russia in the year 1867.

8. Theodore Roosevelt became the president when President _____ was assassinated.

9. Puerto Ricans are citizens of what country? _____

10. During the early part of the _____ War, England favored the southern or Confederate states.

11. President _____ was assassinated by John Wilkes Booth.

12. The _____ Amendment gave the Negroes citizenship and protection under the law.

13. The _____ Amendment abolished slavery in the United States.

14. President William McKinley signed a treaty in 1898 to annex _____, which protected the interests of American investors in sugar plantations.

15. The term _____ refers to the idea of securing recognition and power by investing money in foreign undertakings.

Short Essay Questions. (40 points)

Essay answers are to be written in complete sentences. Each answer is worth four points. Think of the best possible answer before you write.

1. Explain in your own words what the meanings of carpetbaggers and scalawags are.

2. Explain what the Emancipation Proclamation was and what the results of it were.

3. Explain what is meant by the Missouri Compromise.

4. For what main purpose was the Civil War fought?

5. Who was General Sherman?

6. What was the Battle of Gettysburg?

7. What is meant by the term Imperialism?

8. Explain the "open-door" policy with China.

9. Tell what the Monroe Doctrine is, and what the "Roosevelt Corollary" means.

10. Explain what is meant by the term "Big Stick Policy".

Second Quarter Science Exam
Science in God's World 7
Grade 7

Name _____

Directions: on the blank line, write the letter preceding the word or expression that best completes the statement

_____ 1. The water that the body needs in one day would fill about
    a. one glass   c. five glasses
    b. three glasses   d. eight glasses

_____ 2. Foods which supply the energy the body needs contain
    a. vitamins   c. minerals
    b. carbohydrates and fats   d. protein

_____ 3. Another name for vitamin B2 is
    a. riboflavin   c. ascorbic acid
    b. thiamin   d. niacin

_____ 4. A vitamin that must be eaten daily because the body cannot store it
    a. vitamin A   c. vitamin B2
    b. vitamin B1   d. vitamin C

_____ 5. A vitamin that is added to milk by irradiation is
    a. vitamin A   c. vitamin B2
    b. vitamin B1   d. vitamin D

_____ 6. A rough or coarse material in food which helps the digestive system by providing bulk is
    a. minerals   c. roughage
    b. protein   d. grit

_____ 7. Tubes that carry blood away from the heart are called
    a. capillaries   c. arteries
    b. veins   d. conduit

_____ 8. Tubes that carry blood back to the heart are called
    a. veins   c. capillaries
    b. arteries   d. conduit

_____ 9. In the lungs, the blood releases
    a. carbon dioxide gas   c. hydrogen gas
    b. carbon monoxide gas   d. oxygen gas

_____ 10. The heart muscle beats about
    a. 50 times per minute   c. 70 times per minute
    b. 60 times per minute   d. 80 times per minute

_____ 11. Waste materials from the body cells make their way into the blood system by passing through the
   a. capillary walls   c. arterial walls
   b. excretory system   d. heart

_____ 12. The heart muscle is divided into
   a. two chambers   c. four chambers
   b. three chambers   d. six chambers

_____ 13. The study of plants is known as
   a. biology   c. zoology
   b. botany   d. agronomy

_____ 14. The Swedish naturalist who developed a system for classifying plants and animals was
   a. Carl Lief   c. Gregor Mendel
   b. Nils Linnaeus   d. Carl Linnaeus

_____ 15. In the name *Ranunculus lapponicus*, *Ranunculus* refers to the
   a. order   c. genus
   b. family   d. species

_____ 16. In the name *Ranunculus recurvatus*, *recurvatus* refers to the
   a. order   c. genus
   b. family   d. species

_____ 17. The language used by the Linnaean classification system to name plant and animal life is
   a. Greek   c. Hebrew
   b. Latin   d. Swedish

_____ 18. Plants that have roots, stems, leaves, and either flowers or cones are called
   a. thallophytes   c. spermatophytes
   b. bryophytes   d. pteridophytes

_____ 19. Plants that produce their own seeds and live for only one year are
   a. perennials   c. semi-annuals
   b. biennials   d. annuals

_____ 20. Plants that live on from year to year are called
   a. annuals   c. perennials
   b. biennials   d. woody plants

_____ 21. Conifers are examples of
   a. angiosperms   c. gymnosperms
   b. annuals   d. biennials

_____ 22. Fruits and berries are examples of
    a. gymnosperms   c. annuals
    b. angiosperms   d. biennials

_____ 23. The seed and its food supply together form a
    a. husk   c. shell
    b. conglomerate   d. cotyledon

_____ 24. The peanut vine is a
    a. monocot   c. thallophyte
    b. dicot   d. bryophyte

_____ 25. The part of the flower that makes the seed is called the
    a. ovules   c. stamen
    b. pistil   d. pollen

_____ 26. The part of the plant that develops into a seed is the
    a. stamen   c. ovule
    b. pollen   d. pistil

_____ 27. The ripened seed, seed food, and seed case of a plant is known as
    a. the sapling   c. produce
    b. the fruit   d. a pod

_____ 28. A single flower that has its own pistil and stamen
    a. must be a pteridophyte   c. must be a perennial
    b. can self-pollinate   d. cannot self-pollinate

_____ 29. The part of a leaf that takes in carbon dioxide from the air and gives off oxygen and moisture is called
    a. the stomata   c. the blade
    b. the fronds   d. the stalk

_____ 30. The process by which green plants make food is called
    a. pollination   c. transpiration
    b. photosynthesis   d. germination

_____ 31. Plants that do not have seeds are known as
    a. thallophytes   c. pteridophytes
    b. bryophytes   d. all of the above

_____ 32. The green substance in plant cells used in the leaf to make food is
    a. chlorophyll   c. chloroform
    b. hemoglobin   d. sap

_____ 33. Plants that have no chlorophyll and cannot make their own food are
    a. mosses   c. lichens
    b. algae   d. fungi

_____ 34. Bacteria, the tiniest of all plants, are classified according to their
      a. size   c. internal structure
      b. shape   d. threat to human health

_____ 35. Bacteria reproduce by means of
      a. spores   c. cell division
      b. seeds   d. none of the above

_____ 36. Any animal or plant that gets its food from another living animal or plant is called a
      a. scavenger   c. host
      b. parasite   d. guest

_____ 37. The process of absorbing nitrogen from the air by bacteria so that the nitrogen can be used by plants is known as
      a. photosynthesis   c. nitrogen fixation
      b. nitrogen condensation   d. nitrogen transpiration

_____ 38. Simple plants that do not have true leaves, stems, roots, or flowers, but have chlorophyll are known as
      a. liverworts   c. lichens
      b. fungi   d. algae

_____ 39. Plants formed when a fungus and an alga grow together to form one plant are known as
      a. lichens   c. liverworts
      b. mosses   d. Horsetails

_____ 40. An example of a fungus is
      a. a mushroom   c. mold
      b. yeast   d. all of the above

_____ 41. Mushrooms reproduce by means of
      a. cell division   c. spores
      b. seeds   d. none of the above

_____ 42. The leaves of a fern are called
      a. fronds   c. spore cases
      b. petals   d. cones

_____ 43. A waxy material protects the leaves, stems, and roots of some plants from
      a. drying out   c. animals
      b. insects   d. getting too wet

_____ 44. A series of living creatures in which each provides food for the creature next in the series is known as
      a. the survival chain   c. survival of the fittest
      b. supply and demand   d. the food chain

_____ 45. Colonies of tiny plant and animal creatures that live in the ocean are known as
   a. swarms
   b. schools
   c. plankton
   d. flocks

_____ 46. A natural community made up of creatures that live in the ocean is
   a. the aqueous community
   b. the oceanic community
   c. the marine community
   d. the salt-water league

_____ 47. The French scientist who worked with bacteria
   a. Gregor Mendel
   b. Louis Pasteur
   c. Luther Burbank
   d. John Muir

_____ 48. The Austrian abbot who learned how to improve plants by selecting the best seeds from plants that he raised in his garden
   a. Gregor Mendel
   b. John Muir
   c. Louis Pasteur
   d. Luther Burbank

_____ 49. The American naturalist who helped establish Sequoia and Yosemite National Parks as part of a national conservation program
   a. Gregor Mendel
   b. John Muir
   c. Luther Burbank
   d. Louis Pasteur

_____ 50. The American botanist who produced new kinds of plants by cross-pollination
   a. Luther Burbank
   b. John Muir
   c. Gregor Mendel
   d. Louis Pasteur

Grade 7
Third
Quarter

Subject	Monday	Tuesday	Wednesday
Religion	-BH: p. 199-206		-LMR7: p. 127-134
Logic & Spelling	-ICR: p. 120-122 -SF: p. 99-102, L. 17	-SF: p. 103-104	-ICR: p. 123-124
Grammar	-SJG7: p. 315-318 (Stop at "Distributive and Indefinite Pronouns")	-SJG7WB: p. 86	-SJG7WB: p. 87
Reading	-G: p. 176-189	-G: p. 190-204	
History		-GON: Read p. 282-290 -GONWB: p. 71	-GON: Read p. 290-296 -GONWB: p. 72
Math	-SM7: L. 70	-SMTW7: Test 13	-SM7: Investigation 7
Science			
Music Theory			-DMIB: p. 21

Week 19

Subject	Thursday	Friday	Comments
Religion		-BH: p. 206-212	
Logic & Spelling	-SF: Administer pre-test. Student writes words in Spelling notebook 3x each that are wrong.	-SF: Take Post-test for grade.	
Grammar	-SJG7WB: p. 88	-SJG7WB: p. 89	
Reading	-G: p. 205-221		
History			
Math	-SM7: L. 71	-SM7: L. 72 -SMTW7: FPT N	
Science	-SGW7: Read p. 179-188	-SGW7WB: p. 19	
Music Theory			

Week 19

Week 20

Subject	Monday	Tuesday	Wednesday
Religion	-BH: p. 213-218		-LMR7: p. 134-139
Logic & Spelling	-ICR: p.125-127 -SF: p. 105-108, L. 18	-SF: p. 109-110	-ICR: p. 128
Grammar	-SJG7: p. 318-322 (Stop at "2. Uses of Should & Would")	-SJG7WB: p. 90	-SJG7WB: p. 91
Reading	-G: p. 222-234	-G: p. 235-248 (end!) Book report	
History		-GON: Read p. 297-301 -GONWB: p. 73	-GON: Read p. 301-307 -GONWB: p. 74-75
Math	-SM7: L. 73 -SMTW7: FPT O	-SM7: L. 74	-SM7: L. 75
Science			
Music Theory			-DM1B: p. 22

Week 20

Subject	Thursday	Friday	Comments
Religion		-BH: p. 219-225	
Logic & Spelling	-SF: Administer pre-test. Student writes words in Spelling notebook 3x each that are wrong.	-SF: Take Post-test for grade.	
Grammar	-SJG7WB: p. 92	-SJG7WB: p. 93	
Reading	-FW: p. 1-6		
History			
Math	-SMTW7: Test 14	-SM7: L. 76	
Science	-SGW7: Read p. 188-196	-SGW7WB: p. 20	
Music Theory			

Subject	Monday	Tuesday	Wednesday
Religion	-BH: p. 225-231		-LMR7: p. 140-144
Logic & Spelling	-ICR: p. 129 -SF: p. 111-114, L. 19	-SF: p. 115-116	-ICR: p. 130-133
Grammar	-SJG7: p. 323-331	-SJG7WB: p. 94	-SJG7WB: p. 95
Reading	-FW: p. 7-12	-FW: p. 13-18	
History		-GONWB: p. 76	-GON: p. 307-310 Unit Tests (optional extra credit)
Math	-SM7: L. 77	-SM7: L. 78	-SM7: L. 79 -SMTW7: FPT P
Science			
Music Theory			-DM1B: p. 23

Week 21

Week 21

Subject	Thursday	Friday	Comments
Religion		-BH: p. 231-236	
Logic & Spelling	-SF: Administer pre-test. Student writes words in Spelling notebook 3x each that are wrong.	-SF: Take Post-test for grade.	
Grammar	-SJG7WB: p. 96	-SJG7WB: p. 97-98	
Reading	-FW: p. 19-30		
History			
Math	-SM7: L. 80	-SMTW7: Test 15	
Science	-SGW7: Read p. 196-214	-SGW7WB: p. 21	
Music Theory			

Subject	Monday	Tuesday	Wednesday
Religion	-BH: p. 237-242		-LMR7: p. 145-151
Logic & Spelling	-ICR: p. 134-139 -SF: p. 117-120, L. 20	-SF: p. 121-122	-ICR: p. 140-142
Grammar	-SJG7: p. 332-337 (Stop at "Conjunctive Adverbs")	-SJG7WB: p. 99	-SJG7WB: p. 100 (p. 101 extra credit)
Reading	-FW: p. 31-35	-FW: p. 36-42	
History		-GON: Read p. 312-319 -GONWB: p. 77	-GON: Read p. 319-325 -GONWB: p. 78-79
Math	-SM7: Investigation 8	-SM7: L. 81	-SM7: L. 82 -SMTW7: FPT Q
Science			
Music Theory			-DM1B: p. 24

Week 22

Subject	Thursday	Friday	Comments
Religion		-BH: p. 243-248	
Logic & Spelling	-SF: Administer pre-test. Student writes words in Spelling notebook 3x each that are wrong.	-SF: Take Post-test for grade.	
Grammar	-SJG7WB: p. 102	-SJG7WB: p. 103	
Reading	-FW: p. 43-50		
History			
Math	-SM7: L. 83	-SM7: L. 84 -SMTW7: FPT R	
Science	-SGW7: Read p. 214-222	-SGW7WB: p. 22	
Music Theory			

Week 23

Subject	Monday	Tuesday	Wednesday
Religion	-BH: p. 248-255		-LMR7: p. 151-162
Logic & Spelling	-ICR: p. 143-144 SF: p. 123-126, L. 21	-SF: p. 127-128	-ICR: p. 145-147
Grammar	-SJG7: p. 337-343 (Stop at "The Correct Use of Adverbs")	-SJG7WB: p. 104	-SJG7WB: p. 105
Reading	-FW: p. 51-59	-FW: p. 60-69	
History		-GON: Read p. 326-336 -GONWB: p. 80	-GON: Read p. 336-343 -GONWB: p. 81-82
Math	-SM7: L. 85	-SMTW7: Test 16	-SM7: L. 86
Science			
Music Theory			-DM1B: p. 25

Week 23

Subject	Thursday	Friday	Comments
Religion		-BH: p. 255-261	
Logic & Spelling	-SF: Administer pre-test. Student writes words in Spelling notebook 3x each that are wrong.	-SF: Take Post-test for grade.	
Grammar	-SJG7WB: p. 106	-SJG7WB: p. 107	
Reading	-FW: p. 70-75		
History			
Math	-SM7: L. 87	-SM7: L. 88	
Science	-SGW7: Read p. 222-238	-SGW7WB: p. 23	
Music Theory			

Week 24

Subject	Monday	Tuesday	Wednesday
Religion	-BH: p. 261-268		-LMR7: p. 163-169
Logic & Spelling	-ICR: p. 148-151 -SF: p. 129-132, L. 22	-SF: p. 133-134	-ICR: p. 152-155
Grammar	-SJG7: p. 343-347	-SJG7WB: p. 108	-SJG7WB: p. 109
Reading	-FW: p. 76-84	-FW: p. 85-94	
History		-GONWB: p. 83	-GON: p. 344-346 Unit Tests (optional extra credit)
Math	-SM7: L. 89	-SM7: L. 90	-SMTW7: Test 17
Science			
Music Theory			-DM1B: p. 26

Subject	Thursday	Friday	Comments
Religion		-BH: p. 268-275	
Logic & Spelling	-SF: Administer pre-test. Student writes words in Spelling notebook 3x each that are wrong.	-SF: Take Post-test for grade.	
Grammar	-SJG7WB: p. 110	-SJG7WB: p. 111 (p. 112 extra credit)	
Reading	-FW: p. 95-106		
History			
Math	-SM7: Investigation 9	-SM7: L. 91	
Science	-SGW7: Read p. 243-254	-SGW7WB: p. 24	
Music Theory			

Subject	Monday	Tuesday	Wednesday
Religion	-BH: p. 275-280		-LMR7: p. 169-176
Logic & Spelling	-ICR: p. 156-159 -SF: p. 135-138, L. 23	-SF: p. 139-140	-ICR: p. 160-164
Grammar	-SJG7: p. 348-356 (Stop at "Subordinate Conjunctions")	-SJG7WB: p. 113	-SJG7WB: p. 114
Reading	-FW: p. 107-117	-FW: p. 118-127	
History		-GON: Read p. 348-363	-GONWB: p. 84-85
Math	-SM7: L. 92	-SM7: L. 93	-SM7: L. 94 -SMTW7: FPT S
Science			
Music Theory			-DM1B: p. 27

Week 25

Subject	Thursday	Friday	Comments
Religion		-BH: p. 281-286	
Logic & Spelling	-SF: Administer pre-test. Student writes words in Spelling notebook 3x each that are wrong.	-SF: Take Post-test for grade.	
Grammar	-SJG7WB: p. 115	-SJG7WB: p. 116	
Reading	-FW: p. 128-139		
History			
Math	SM7: L. 95	-SMTW7: Test 18	
Science	-SGW7: Read p. 254-266	-SGW7WB: p. 25	
Music Theory			

Week 26

Subject	Monday	Tuesday	Wednesday
Religion	-BH: p. 286-292		-LMR7: p. 176-180
Logic & Spelling	-ICR: p. 165-168 -SF: p. 141-144, L. 24	-SF: p. 145-146	-ICR: p. 169-170
Grammar	-SJG7: p. 356-360	-SJG7WB: p. 117	-SJG7WB: p. 118
Reading	-FW: p. 140-146	-FW: p. 147-154	
History		-GON: Read p. 363-377	-GONWB: p. 86
Math	-SM7: L. 96	-SM7: L. 97 -SMTW7: FPT T	-SM7: L. 98
Science			
Music Theory			-DM1B: p. 28

Week 26

Subject	Thursday	Friday	Comments
Religion		-BH: p. 292-298	
Logic & Spelling	-SF: Administer pre-test. Student writes words in Spelling notebook 3x each that are wrong.	-SF: Take Post-test for grade.	
Grammar	-SJG7WB: p. 119	-SJG7WB: p. 120	
Reading	-FW: p. 155-163		
History			
Math	-SM7: L. 99	-SM7: L. 100	
Science	-SGW7: p. 266-277 (Teacher may want to mention about how superstitions with the zodiac are sinful and silly)	-SGW7WB: p. 26	
Music Theory			

Week 27

Subject	Monday	Tuesday	Wednesday
Religion	-BH: p. 298-303		-LMR7: p. 181-191
Logic & Spelling	-ICR: Review p. 169-170		-ICR: p. 171-172
Grammar	-SJG7: p. 361-369	-SJG7WB: p. 121	-SJG7WB: p. 122 (p. 123 extra credit)
Reading	-FW: p. 164-175	-FW: p. 176-181	
History		-GON: Study for Third Quarter Exam (Ch. 15-19)	
Math	-SMTW7: Test 19	-SM7: Investigation 10 -SMTW7: Activity Sheet 7	-SM7: L. 101
Science			
Music Theory			-DM1B: p. 29

Week 27			
Subject	Thursday	Friday	Comments
Religion		BH: p. 304-309	
Logic & Spelling			
Grammar	-SJG7WB: p. 124 (p. 125 extra credit)	-SJG7WB: p. 126	
Reading	-FW: p. 182-191		
History	-Third Quarter Exam (remove 2 pages from here)		
Math	-SM7: L. 102	-SM7: L. 103 -SMTW7: FPT U	
Science	-SGW7: Study for Third Quarter Exam (p. 179-278)	-Third Quarter Exam (remove 6 pages from here)	
Music Theory			

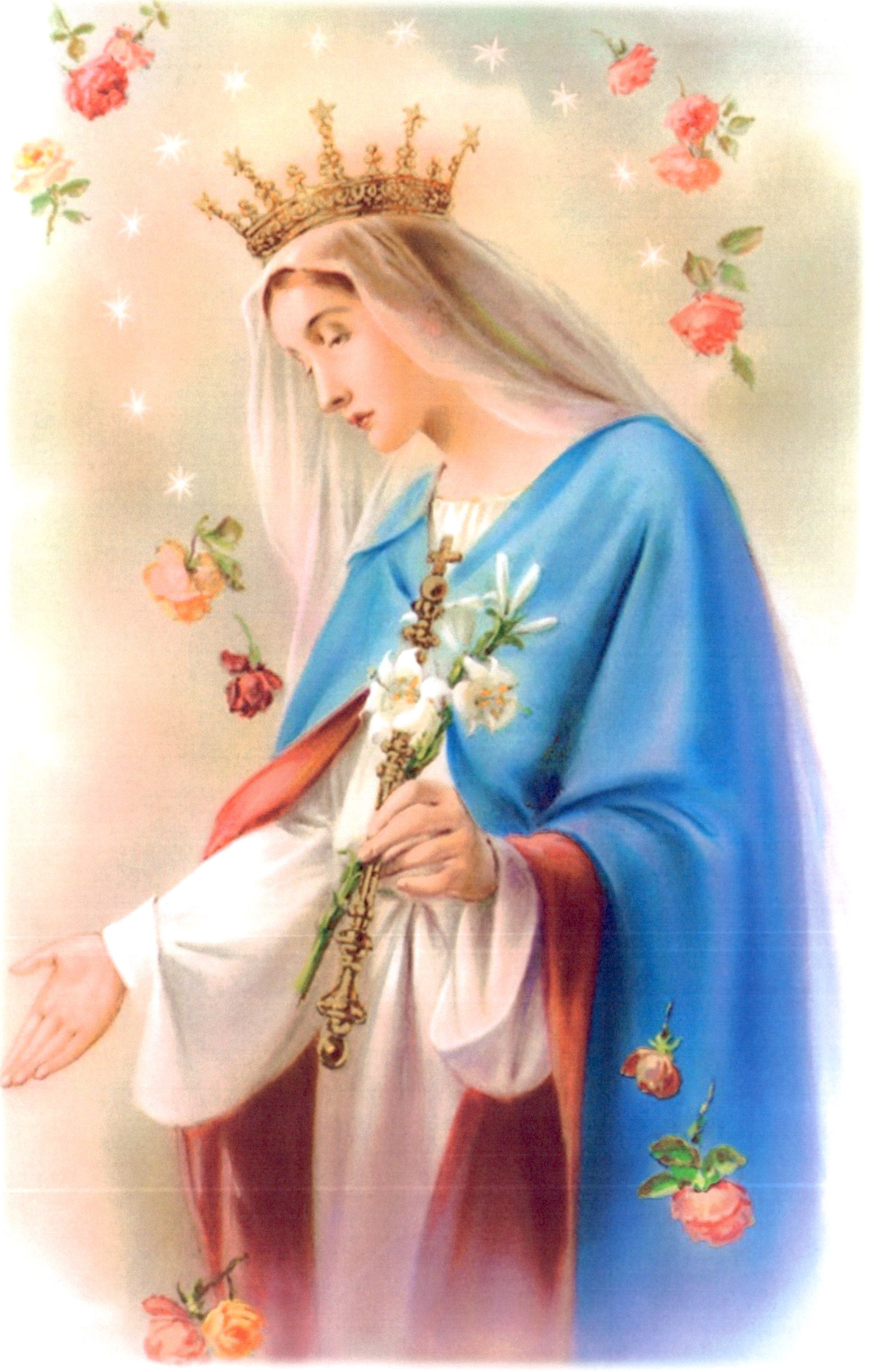

Third Quarter History Exam
The Growth of Our Nation
Grade 7

Name _____

True or False (40 points)

1. _____ Greenbacks were issued during the Revolutionary War.

2. _____ Andrew Jackson claimed that the Bank of the United States was a great blessing for the people.

3. _____ Alexander Hamilton established the credit of the United States.

4. _____ The Fourteenth Amendment gave Congress the power to levy an income tax.

5. _____ Many persons seeking employment by the federal government are required to take a civil-service examination.

6. _____ The Federalists were the first political party.

7. _____ The name of the bridge across San Francisco Bay is called the Oakland Bay Bridge.

8. _____ The Legion of Decency rates motion pictures and indicates which are objectionable on moral grounds.

9. _____ The first gasoline engine for automobiles was made by a German.

10. _____ The first message sent by the telegraph was "What God hath wrought."

11. _____ President Jackson withdrew government deposits and placed them in specially picked state banks nicknamed, "pet banks".

12. _____ The "Crime of '73" involved the demonetization of silver.

13. _____ After the "Crime of '73", silver was never used for United States coinage again.

14. _____ A revenue tariff is a tariff placed on goods to protect home manufacturers from the competition of foreign manufacturers.

15. _____ A protective tariff is a tariff placed to obtain money for the expenses of government.

16. _____ In the early 1800s there were many opposing views on tariff laws.

17. _____ The term "universal manhood suffrage" includes women in the right to vote.

18. _____ Only the federal government of the United States can coin money, declare war, and establish post offices.

19. _____ National election day is set as the Tuesday following the first Monday in November.

20. _____ The telegraph made no difference in American life.

Fill in the Blanks (some will not be used) (40 points):

Peter Cooper	meat	Granger Laws
George Washington	gutta-percha	toes
free trade	1812	tobacco
1254	Gold Standard	15th
judicial	Tariff of Abominations	12th
tariff	Woodrow Wilson	Marconi
initiative	mayor	Henry Clay
Phoenicians	money	Charles Goodyear

1. A bank is an establishment for keeping, lending or exchanging _____.

2. The War of _____ encouraged American manufacturing as it forced us to produce many of the goods that were formerly imported such as cotton and woolen goods, glass, and pottery.

3. The Federal Reserve System was established during the administration of _____.

4. The early American colonists often used _____ as money.

5. With the passage of the _____ Act in 19000, the United States adopted gold as the single standard of money.

6. The _____ branch of our government interprets the laws.

7. A young Italian scientist, _____, invented the wireless telegraph.

8. Instead of a king, the Constitution provides for a president chosen by the people. _____ was our first president.

9. The head of the city government is usually the _____ who is elected by popular vote.

10. The _____ were the first to develop an alphabet.

11. A _____ is a tax placed on goods imported or brought into a country from foreign countries.

12. A policy that places no taxes on foreign goods which are not produced within our country is called _____.

13. The _____ of 1828 placed taxes on imported goods at outrageously high rates, and resulted in the Ordinance of Nullification of 1832.

14. In 1833, _____ proposed a compromise which gradually lowered the taxes on imported goods.

15. The _____ Amendment gave Negroes the right to vote in 1870.

16. Citizens of the United States have the power to propose new laws or suggest an amendment to the state constitution by preparing a special petition, obtaining the required number of signatures, and then voting on the proposed law or amendment. This procedure is called _____.

17. A thick, milky juice that became waterproof when it hardened and made the Atlantic cable possible was called _____.

18. An American named _____ invented the process of vulcanizing rubber.

19. _____ built the first steam locomotive called the Tom Thumb, which operated on the B&O Railroad, carrying 24 passengers at a speed of 4 miles an hour.

20. In the years 1870-1875, _____ were passed to correct railroad abuses, establish fixed rates, and enforce new laws regulating railroads.

Short Essay Questions. (20 points)

Essay answers are to be written in complete sentences. Each answer is worth four points. Think of the best possible answer before you write.

1. The federal government is composed of three branches. Name each branch and state its purpose.

_____

_____

_____

_____

_____

2. Who were the Wright brothers and why were they famous?

_____

_____

3. Explain what Morse code is.

4. Who invented the telephone? Tell a little about his background.

5. Why is Henry Ford famous?

Third Quarter Science Exam
Science in God's World 7
Grade 7

Name _____

Directions: on the blank line, write the letter preceding the word or expression that best completes the statement

_____ 1. The temperature of the sun at its surface is about
    a. 120°F
    b. 1,200°F
    c. 12,000°F
    d. 120,000°F

_____ 2. Substances like sodium, oxygen, iron, and copper are examples of
    a. compounds
    b. elements
    c. mixtures
    d. solutions

_____ 3. The German scientist who invented the spectroscope and discovered that each element gives off its own special color of light when heated enough was
    a. Ludwig von Beethoven
    b. Albert Einstein
    c. Johannes Kepler
    d. Joseph von Fraunhofer

_____ 4. The law of conservation of energy states that
    a. matter can be created or destroyed
    b. energy can be created or destroyed
    c. energy cannot be created or destroyed
    d. certain conditions always produce the same results

_____ 5. The heat and light from the sun travel towards the earth at a speed of
    a. 186,000 miles per hour
    b. 186,000 miles per second
    c. 246,000 miles per hour
    d. 246,000 miles per second

_____ 6. Heat rays from the sun are absorbed best by
    a. solids
    b. liquids
    c. gases
    d. plasma

_____ 7. Heat is measured in
    a. calories
    b. degrees
    c. minutes
    d. lumens

_____ 8. Temperature is measured in
    a. centimeters
    b. degrees
    c. meters
    d. calories

_____ 9. The boiling point of water is
    a. 0°C   b. 32°C   c. 100°C   d. 212°C

_____ 10. The number of degrees between the boiling point and the freezing point of water on the Fahrenheit scale is
    a. 100   b. 180   c. 212   d. 273

_____ 11. When an object is heated, its molecules
    a. decompose
    b. move slower
    c. stop moving
    d. move faster

_____ 12. The amount of heat required to raise one gram of water one degree centigrade is
    a. the freezing point of water
    b. the boiling point of water
    c. one calorie
    d. one degree Fahrenheit

_____ 13. The combining of oxygen with any other material is called
    a. reduction
    b. oxidation
    c. halogenation
    d. hydrogenation

_____ 14. Another name for hard coal is
    a. peat
    b. lignite
    c. bituminous
    d. anthracite

_____ 15. The law of conservation of matter states that
    a. matter can be either created or destroyed
    b. energy can be either created or destroyed
    c. matter can be neither created or destroyed
    d. energy can be neither created or destroyed

_____ 16. Friction produces
    a. chemical energy
    b. light energy
    c. mechanical energy
    d. heat energy

_____ 17. Any material that allows heat and electricity to easily pass through is
    a. an insulator
    b. a conductor
    c. a non-metal
    d. radioactive

_____ 18. A device to produce usable amounts of heat by concentrating the sun's rays is called
    a. a solar heater
    b. a solar system
    c. a solarium
    d. a solar panel

_____ 19. As a substance becomes hotter
    a. the molecules stop moving
    b. the molecules move closer together
    c. the molecules move more slowly
    d. the molecules move farther apart

_____ 20. As water is cooled from 39°F to 32°F,
    a. it expands
    b. it contracts
    c. its volume does not change
    d. its molecules move more rapidly

_____ 21. Thermostats contain a
    a. bar of silver
    b. bimetal bar
    c. bar of iron
    d. bar of steel

_____ 22. The process of changing a vapor to a liquid is called
    a. fusion
    b. evaporation
    c. melting
    d. condensation

_____ 23. The process of changing a liquid to a vapor is called
    a. evaporation
    b. condensation
    c. melting
    d. freezing

_____ 24. A change in state is always accompanied by a change in
    a. light energy
    b. temperature
    c. heat energy
    d. substance

_____ 25. Whenever a gas changes to a liquid, or a liquid to a solid,
    a. heat energy has been added to the substance
    b. heat energy has been taken away from the substance
    c. there is no change in total heat content in the substance
    d. a change of state has not occurred

_____ 26. The transfer of heat by the circulation of heated particles of a gas or liquid is
    a. convection
    b. conduction
    c. radiation
    d. heat exchange

_____ 27. The transfer of heat from one substance to another by contact is
    a. radiation
    b. conduction
    c. convection
    d. heat exchange

_____ 28. The sun warms the earth by means of
    a. convection
    b. conduction
    c. radiation
    d. exchange

_____ 29. Most of the heat energy from a radiant body like the sun comes in the form of
    a. x-rays
    b. visible waves
    c. ultraviolet waves
    d. infrared waves

_____ 30. When two solid objects at different temperatures come into contact with one another
    a. heat is transferred by convection
    b. heat is transferred from the cooler object to the warmer object
    c. heat is transferred from the warmer object to the cooler object
    d. heat is transferred by radiation

_____ 31. The belief that the sun and planets orbit around the earth is referred to as
    a. geocentrism
    b. galaxy
    c. lunar system
    d. heliocentrism

_____ 32. The belief that the earth and planets orbit around the sun is referred to as
    a. geocentrism
    b. nebular theory
    c. heliocentrism
    d. constellation myth

_____ 33. A group or system of billions of stars is called a
    a. solar system
    b. nebulae
    c. constellation
    d. galaxy

_____ 34. A star that suddenly becomes brighter, then fades is known as a
    a. regular star
    b. nebulae
    c. variable star
    d. nova

_____ 35. Stars that change magnitude in a regular pattern are called
    a. variable stars
    b. regular stars
    c. constellations
    d. gaseous nebulae

_____ 36. The star *Sirius* has an absolute magnitude of +1.4, *Alpha Centauri* has an absolute magnitude of +4.4, *Antares* has an absolute magnitude of -4.3. Which star is the brightest?
    a. Sirius
    b. Alpha Centauri
    c. Antares
    d. all stars are equally bright

_____ 37. The Dutch lens maker who invented the first refracting telescope was
    a. Galileo Galilei
    b. Hans Lippershey
    c. Nicholas Copernicus
    d. Urbain Leverrier

_____ 38. The Danish astronomer who first calculated the speed of light to be 192,000 miles per second was
    a. Hans Lippershey
    b. Albert Michelson
    c. Carlus Linnaeus
    d. Olaus Roemer

_____ 39. The English scientist who said that gravitational force increases with the size of the objects and with their nearness to one another was
    a. Hans Lippershey
    b. Johannes Kepler
    c. Olaus Roemer
    d. Sir Isaac Newton

_____ 40. The French astronomer who predicted the size and location of Uranus before it was actually discovered was
    a. Hans Lippershey
    b. Sir Isaac Newton
    c. Johannes Kepler
    d. Urbain Leverrier

_____ 41. A cloud of gas seen among the heavenly bodies is known as a
    a. gaseous nebula
    b. spiral nebula
    c. nova
    d. supernova

_____ 42. A galaxy of stars so distant that it looks like a gaseous nebula is known as a
    a. gaseous nebula
    b. spiral nebula
    c. nova
    d. supernova

_____ 43. Earth is on the outer edge of a galaxy called
    a. Cancer
    b. the Big Dipper
    c. Pisces
    d. the Milky Way

_____ 44. Our galaxy is shaped like a _____ 110,000 light-years across.
    a. sphere
    b. cube
    c. disc or wheel
    d. cone

_____ 45. The stars and planets would fly away from the center of the galaxy into space if it were not for the
    a. force of gravitation
    b. Little Dipper
    c. dark nebulae
    d. closer constellations

_____ 46. The Big Dipper is really part of a much larger constellation called
    a. Ursa Major, or the Big Bear
    b. Ursa Minor, or Little Bear
    c. Draco, or the Dragon
    d. Taurus, or the Bull

_____ 47. The point where the earth and sky seem to meet is called the
    a. horizon
    b. zenith
    c. zodiac
    d. peak

_____ 48. The point in the heavens directly overhead is called
    a. horizon
    b. zenith
    c. zodiac
    d. canopy

_____ 49. The path that the sun appears to follow among the stars is called
    a. the equator
    b. the ellipse
    c. the eclipse
    d. the ecliptic

_____ 50. On any one night, you should be able to see
    a. five constellations
    b. six constellations
    c. seven constellations
    d. eight constellations

Grade 7 Fourth Quarter

Week 28

Subject	Monday	Tuesday	Wednesday
Religion	-BH: p. 310-315		-LMR7: p. 191-198
Logic & Spelling	-ICR: p. 173 -SF: p. 147-150, L. 25	-SF: p. 151-152	-ICR: p. 174-175
Grammar	-SJG7: p. 370-373	-SJG7WB: p. 127	-SJG7WB: p. 128
Reading	-FW: p. 192-201	-FW: p. 202-207	-FW: p. 208-216
History		-GON: Read p. 378-389 -GONWB: p. 87-88	-GON: Read p. 389-400 -GONWB: p. 89
Math	-SM7: L. 104	-SM7: L. 105	-SMTW7: Test 20
Science			
Music Theory			-DM1B: p. 30

Week 28

Subject	Thursday	Friday	Comments
Religion		-BH: p. 315-320	
Logic & Spelling	-SF: Administer pre-test. Student writes words in Spelling notebook 3x each that are wrong.	-SF: Take Post-test for grade.	
Grammar	-SJG7WB: p. 129	-SJG7WB: p. 130	
Reading	-FW: p. 217-229		
History			
Math	-SM7: L. 106	-SM7: L. 107 -SMTW7: Activity Sheet 8	
Science	-SGW7: Read p. 278-290	-SGW7WB: p. 27	
Music Theory			

Week 29

Subject	Monday	Tuesday	Wednesday
Religion	-BH: p. 321-326		-LMR7: p. 198-205
Logic & Spelling	-ICR: p. 176 -SF: p. 153-156, L. 26	-SF: p. 157-158	-ICR: p. 177-178
Grammar	-SJG7: p. 374-378 (Stop at "Complex Sentences")	-SJG7WB: p. 131	-SJG7WB: p. 132
Reading	-FW: p. 230-238	-FW: p. 239-244	-FW: p. 245-253
History		-GON: Read p. 400-406 -GONWB: p. 90	-GON: Read p. 407-414 -GONWB: p. 91
Math	-SM7: L. 108 -SMTW7: FPT V	-SM7: L. 109	-SM7: L. 110
Science			
Music Theory			-DM1B: p. 31

Week 29

Subject	Thursday	Friday	Comments
Religion		-BH: p. 326-332	
Logic & Spelling	-SF: Administer pre-test. Student writes words in Spelling notebook 3x each that are wrong.	-SF: Take Post-test for grade.	
Grammar	-SJG7WB: p. 133	-SJG7WB: p. 134	
Reading	-FW: p. 254-262		
History	-GON: Read p. 414-420 -GONWB: p. 92-93		
Math	-SMTW7: Test 21	-SM7: Investigation 11 -SMTW7: Activity Sheets 9-11	
Science	-SGW7: Read p. 290-299	-SGW7WB: p. 28	
Music Theory			

Week 30

Subject	Monday	Tuesday	Wednesday
Religion	-BH: p. 332-339		-LMR7: p. 205-214
Logic & Spelling	-ICR: p. 179 -SF: p. 159-162, L. 27	-SF: p. 163-164	-ICR: p. 180
Grammar	-SJG7: p. 378-384 (Stop at "2. Adverbial Clauses")	-SJG7WB: p. 135	-SJG7WB: p. 136
Reading	-FW: p. 263-269 (end!) Book report	-SJBS: p. 1-8 (about 5 stories a day)	-SJBS: p. 8-15
History		-GONWB: p. 94-95	-GON: p. 420-422 Unit Tests (optional extra credit)
Math	-SM7: L. 111	-SM7: L. 112	-SM7: L. 113
Science			
Music Theory			-DM1B: p. 32

Week 30

Subject	Thursday	Friday	Comments
Religion		-BH: p. 339-345	
Logic & Spelling	-SF: Administer pre-test. Student writes words in Spelling notebook 3x each that are wrong.	-SF: Take Post-test for grade.	
Grammar	-SJG7WB: p. 137	-SJG7WB: p. 138	
Reading	-SJBS: p. 15-24		
History			
Math	-SM7: L. 114 -SMTW7: FPT W	-SM7: L. 115	
Science	-SGW7: Read p. 299-308	-SGW7WB: p. 29	
Music Theory			

Subject	Monday	Tuesday	Wednesday
Religion	-BH: p. 346-351		-LMR7: p. 215-220
Logic & Spelling	-ICR: p. 181-183 SF: p. 165-168, L. 28	-SF: p. 169-170	-ICR: 184-188
Grammar	-SJG7: p. 384-389 (Stop at "Noun Clauses Used as Direct Objects")	-SJG7WB: p. 139	-SJG7WB: p. 140
Reading	-SJBS: p. 24-32	-SJBS: p. 32-40	-SJBS: p. 41-53
History		-GON: Read p. 428-436 -GONWB: p. 96-97	-GON: Read p. 436-443 -GONWB: p. 98-99
Math	-SMTW7: Test 22	-SM7: L. 116	-SM7: L. 117
Science			
Music Theory			-DMIB: p. 33

Week 31

Week 31

Subject	Thursday	Friday	Comments
Religion		-BH: p. 352-356	
Logic & Spelling	-SF: Administer pre-test. Student writes words in Spelling notebook 3x each that are wrong.	-SF: Take Post-test for grade.	
Grammar	-SJG7WB: p. 141	-SJG7WB: p. 142	
Reading	-SJBS: p. 53-61		
History			
Math	-SM7: L. 118	-SM7: L. 119	
Science	-SGW7: Read p. 308-312	-SGW7WB: p. 30	
Music Theory			

Week 32

Subject	Monday	Tuesday	Wednesday
Religion	-BH: p. 357-362		-LMR7: p. 220-230
Logic & Spelling	-ICR: p. 189-190 -SF: p. 171-174, L. 29	-SF: p. 175-176	-ICR: p. 191-192
Grammar	-SJG7: p. 389-398	-SJG7WB: p. 143	-SJG7WB: p. 144
Reading	-SJBS: p. 61-68	-SJBS: p. 69-80	-SJBS: p. 80-90
History		-GON: Read p. 444-452 -GONWB: p. 100	-GON: Read p. 452-458 -GONWB: p. 101
Math	-SM7: L. 120	-SMTW7: Test 23	-SM7: Investigation 12 -SMTW7: Activity Sheet 12
Science			
Music Theory			-DM1B: p. 34

Week 32

Subject	Thursday	Friday	Comments
Religion		-BH: p. 362-368	
Logic & Spelling	-SF: Administer pre-test. Student writes words in Spelling notebook 3x each that are wrong.	-SF: Take Post-test for grade.	
Grammar	-SJG7WB: p. 145	-SJG7WB: p. 146	
Reading	-SJBS: p. 90-105		
History			
Math	-SM7: Topic A, p. 855-857 (end!)		
Science	-SGW7: Read p. 317-325	-SGW7WB: p. 31	
Music Theory			

Week 33

Subject	Monday	Tuesday	Wednesday
Religion	-BH: p. 369-374		-LMR7: p. 230-235
Logic & Spelling	-ICR: p. 193-194 -SF: p. 177-180, L. 30	-SF: p. 181-182	-ICR: p. 195-196
Grammar	-SJG7: p. 399-406	-SJG7WB: p. 147	-SJG7WB: p. 148
Reading	-SJBS: p. 106-116	-SJBS: p. 116-125	-SJBS: p. 125-130
History	-Remove Map #1 from the back. Give to student to study*	-GON: Read p. 459-464 -GONWB: p. 102 (skip Section C)	-GON: Read p. 464-472 -GONWB: p. 104-105
Math			
Science			
Music Theory			-DM1B: p. 35

Week 33

Subject	Thursday	Friday	Comments
Religion		-BH: p. 375-382	
Logic & Spelling	-SF: Administer pre-test. Student writes words in Spelling notebook 3x each that are wrong.	-SF: Take Post-test for grade.	
Grammar	-SJG7WB: p. 149	-SJG7WB: p. 150-151 (p. 152 extra credit)	
Reading	-SJBS: p. 131-138		
History			*Show student the list for the test and Map #2 so he knows what to expect on next Monday.
Math			
Science	-SGW7: Read p.325-336	-SGW7WB: p. 32	
Music Theory			

Week 34

Subject	Monday	Tuesday	Wednesday
Religion	-BH: p. 383-388 (end!)		-LMR7: p. 235-242
Logic & Spelling	-ICR: p. 197-198 -SF: p. 183-186, L. 31	-SF: p. 187-188	-ICR: p. 199
Grammar	-SJG7: p. 407-408	-SJG7WB: p. 153	-SJG7WB: p. 154
Reading	-SJBS: p. 139-150	-SJBS: p. 150-158	-SJBS: p. 158-166
History	-Give test with Map #2 and List. This could be just for fun or grade.	-GON: Read p. 472-477 -GONWB: p. 106-107	-GONWB: p. 108-109
Math			
Science			
Music Theory			-DMIB: p. 36

Week 34

Subject	Thursday	Friday	Comments
Religion			
Logic & Spelling	-SF: Administer pre-test. Student writes words in Spelling notebook 3x each that are wrong.	-SF: Take Post-test for grade.	
Grammar	-SJG7WB: p. 155	-SJG7WB: p. 156	
Reading	-SJBS: p. 166-176	-SJBS: p. 176-185	
History			
Math			
Science	-SGW7: Read p. 336-352	-SGW7WB: p. 33	
Music Theory			

Week 35

Subject	Monday	Tuesday	Wednesday
Religion			-LMR7: p. 242-248
Logic & Spelling	-ICR: p. 201-203 -SF: p. 189-192, L. 32	-SF: p. 193-194	-ICR: p. 204-205
Grammar	-SJG7: p. 409-413 (Stop at "The Colon")	-SJG7WB: p. 157	-SJG7WB: p. 158
Reading	-SJBS: p. 185-196	-SJBS: p. 197-205	-SJBS: p. 205-213
History	-Remove Map #3 from the back. Give to student to study*	-GON: p. 478-479 Unit Tests (optional extra credit)	-GON: Read p. 484-492 -GONWB: p. 110-111 (end!)
Math			
Science			
Music Theory			-DM1B: p. 37

Week 35

Subject	Thursday	Friday	Comments
Religion		-LMR7: Student reads p. 250-257 on his own (end!)	
Logic & Spelling	-SF: Administer pre-test. Student writes words in Spelling notebook 3x each that are wrong.	-SF: Take Post-test for grade.	
Grammar	-SJG7WB: p. 159	-SJG7WB: p. 160	
Reading	-SJBS: p. 214-224	-SJBS: p. 224-230	
History	-GON: Read p. 493-511		*Show student the list for the test and Map #4 so he knows what to expect on next Monday.
Math			
Science	-SGW7: Read p. 352-365	-SGW7WB: p. 34	
Music Theory			

Week 36

Subject	Monday	Tuesday	Wednesday
Religion			
Logic & Spelling	-ICR: p. 206-207		-ICR: p. 208-209 (end!)
Grammar	-SJG7: p. 413-420 (end!)	-SJG7WB: p. 161	-SJG7WB: p. 162
Reading	-SJBS: p. 230-239	-SJBS: p. 239-248	-SJBS: p. 248-254
History		-Give test with Map #4 and List. This could be just for fun or grade.	-GON: Study for Fourth Quarter Exam (Ch. 20 – Conclusion)
Math			
Science			
Music Theory			-DM1B: p. 38

Week 36

Subject	Thursday	Friday	Comments
Religion			
Logic & Spelling			
Grammar	-SJG7WB: p. 163-164 (end!)		
Reading	-SJBS: p. 254-264 (end!) Book report		
History	-**Fourth Quarter Exam** (remove 2 pages from here)		
Math			
Science	-SGW7: Study for Third Quarter Exam (p. 278-365)	-**Fourth Quarter Exam** (remove 8 pages from here)	
Music Theory		-Eat a bowl of ice cream and maybe give the student one, too! 😉	

LAST DAY OF SCHOOL

Fourth Quarter History Exam
The Growth of Our Nation
Grade 7

Name _____

True or False (30 points)

_____ 1. Elizabeth was the first woman doctor of modern times.

_____ 2. Austin Flint was the first to use a stethoscope in detecting heart trouble.

_____ 3. The Mayo Clinic is located in North Dakota.

_____ 4. The first bishop of Charleston, South Carolina was Reverend John England.

_____ 5. Mother Seton was the foundress of the Daughters of Charity.

_____ 6. American troops were sent to Haiti because the United States wanted to own this island.

_____ 7. The states of the United States that border Mexico are Texas, New Mexico, and California.

_____ 8. The completion of the Panama Canal took place during the administration of Andrew Jackson.

_____ 9. Booker T. Washington "lifted the veil of ignorance from his people and pointed the way to progress through education and industry."

_____ 10. Louisa M. Alcott, an American writer of the nineteenth century, gave Americans the heartwarming story, "Little Women".

Fill in the Blanks (30 points)

Edison	Jesuits	White Fathers
anthracite	Mexico and Canada	German
Chicago	Leo XIII	potato mush
16th Amendment	13th Amendment	Minnesota
Florida	Legion of Decency	Marcus
Italian	Pasteur	gooey stuff

1. The _____ rated motion pictures and indicated which are objectionable on moral grounds.

2. The first gasoline engine for automobiles was made by a _____.

3. The _____ gave Congress the power to levy an income tax.

4. The richest iron deposit of the world, Mesabi Range, is located in _____.

5. _____ established his workshop and laboratory in Menlo Park, New Jersey.

6. Another name for hard coal is _____.

7. The first hospitals on the North American Continent were established in _____.

8. Georgetown College was entrusted to what Religious order? _____

9. Pope _____ defended the cause of labor in an encyclical.

10. Archbishop Satolli was the Pope's personal representative to the World's Fair held in _____ in the year 1893.

Short Essay Questions. (40 points)

Essay answers are to be written in complete sentences. Each answer is worth four points. Think of the best possible answer before you write.

1. Who were the Wright brothers and what made them famous?

2. Name the three branches of the federal government and their purpose.

3. When the Titanic hit an iceberg in 1912, how were 700 passengers saved from drowning? What major invention prevented the disaster from taking a higher death toll?

4. Tell why coal mining is a dangerous occupation.

5. Archbishop Hughes was the chief foe of Native Americans. Why?

6. Who is the Patroness of the United States and how did this come about?

7. Who was Louis Braille?

8. What do these men have in common: Washington Irving, James Fenimore Cooper, William Cullen Bryant, Nathaniel Hawthorne, and Henry Wadsworth Longfellow?

9. Name at least three pillars of Catholic education from the 1800's.

10. What are some of Thomas Alva Edison's inventions?

Fourth Quarter Science Exam
Science in God's World 7
Grade 7

Name _____

Directions: on the blank line, write the letter preceding the word or expression that best completes the statement

_____ 1. The English scientist and mathematician who suggested the theory of gravitation was
  a. Tycho Brahe   c. Galileo Galilei
  b. Ptolemy   d. Sir Isaac Newton

_____ 2. The sun with its planets, the stars, and the universe revolving around the earth is called the _____ system.
  a. parabolic   c. heliocentric
  b. geocentric   d. linear

_____ 3. The planet closest to the sun is
  a. Mercury   c. Venus
  b. Mars   d. Neptune

_____ 4. Dark spots that appear on the face of the sun are called
  a. prominences   c. solar spots
  b. sunspots   d. solar flares

_____ 5. Any of the many very small planetoids revolving about the sun between the orbit of Mars and the orbit of Jupiter are called
  a. comets   c. meteorites
  b. meteors   d. asteroids

_____ 6. A heavenly body that has a starlike head and a shining tail is a(n)
  a. planetoid   c. meteorites
  b. meteor   d. comet

_____ 7. The Greek scholar who first calculated the circumference of the earth was
  a. Eratosthenes   c. Pythagoras
  b. Archimedes   d. Hippocrates

_____ 8. The 47° that the sun travels down and then another 47° back up again during its spiral-shaped revolution cycle for the duration of the calendar year, is referred to as its
  a. inclination   c. triangulation
  b. annual movement   d. rotation

_____ 9. December 21, the day on which the sun stops its southward movement is called
  a. the spring equinox   c. the fall equinox
  b. the winter solstice   d. a solar eclipse

_____ 10. March 21, one of two days when hours of daylight equal hours of darkness is called
    a. the spring equinox   c. the fall equinox
    b. the winter solstice   d. a solar eclipse

_____ 11. When the moon is between the earth and the sun, the side of the moon that faces the earth is dark. This is called a
    a. new moon   c. full moon
    b. first-quarter moon   d. last-quarter moon

_____ 12. A new moon is followed by a
    a. crescent moon   c. full moon
    b. first-quarter moon   d. last-quarter moon

_____ 13. The distance north or south of the equator measured in degrees is
    a. latitude   c. longitude
    b. a meridian   d. an angle

_____ 14. A circle passing through any place on the earth's surface and through the North and South Poles and used to measure longitude is called
    a. the Tropic of Capricorn   c. the Antarctic Circle
    b. the equator   d. a meridian

_____ 15. In 1884AD, it was agreed that the zero meridian, called the prime meridian would pass through
    a. Berlin, Germany   c. Rome, Italy
    b. Greenwich, England   d. Paris, France

_____ 16. A circle whose diameter passes through the center of the earth is known as
    a. the Tropic of Cancer   c. the equator
    b. a great circle   d. the Arctic Circle

_____ 17. The circle of latitude located 23.5° from the North Pole is called the
    a. Arctic Circle   c. Antarctic Circle
    b. Tropic of Cancer   d. Tropic of Capricorn

_____ 18. The torrid zone is located between the
    a. Tropic of Cancer and the Arctic Circle
    b. Arctic Circle and the Antarctic Circle
    c. Equator and the North Pole
    d. Tropic of Cancer and the Tropic of Capricorn

_____ 19. The equator is numbered as
    a. 0° latitude   c. 180° latitude
    b. 90° latitude   d. 360° latitude

_____ 20. A clock or watch that keeps very accurate time is known as a
    a. time piece   c. chronometer
    b. bolometer   d. barometer

_____ 21. The international date line is located at the
    a. 0° meridian   c. 0° latitude
    b. 180° meridian   d. 180° latitude

_____ 22. Concrete may crack in the winter due to
    a. the cold
    b. the contraction of the molecules which make up the concrete
    c. the contraction of water as it freezes
    d. the expansion of water as it freezes

_____ 23. Iron rusts when the iron atoms combine with oxygen. This process is called
    a. oxidation   c. electrolysis
    b. reduction   d. combustion

_____ 24. When coal is burned it produces
    a. ash   c. liquids and gases
    b. heat and light   d. all of the above

_____ 25. A single particle of water is a(n)
    a. atom   c. molecule
    b. element   d. electron

_____ 26. Molecules can be broken down into smaller particles called
    a. compounds   c. atoms
    b. mixtures   d. solutions

_____ 27. Each molecule of water is made up of
    a. two atoms of hydrogen and one atom of oxygen
    b. two atoms of oxygen and one atom of hydrogen
    c. two atoms of hydrogen and two atoms of oxygen
    d. one atom of oxygen and one atom of hydrogen

_____ 28. Water, table salt, and sugar are examples of
    a. atoms   c. solutions
    b. mixtures   d. compounds

_____ 29. Oxygen, hydrogen, sodium, chlorine, and carbon are examples of
    a. elements   c. compounds
    b. molecules   d. mixtures

_____ 30. The elements platinum, gold, silver, copper, iron, lead, tin, and zinc are examples of
    a. nonmetals   c. metals
    b. insulators   d. compounds

_____ 31. The elements oxygen, hydrogen, helium, nitrogen, sulfur, and phosphorous are examples of
    a. metals
    b. compounds
    c. conductors
    d. nonmetals

_____ 32. The temperature at which a substance changes from a liquid to a gas is called the
    a. melting point
    b. freezing point
    c. boiling point
    d. dew point

_____ 33. The freezing point of a substance is the same as its
    a. dew point
    b. melting point
    c. boiling point
    d. kindling point

_____ 34. At ordinary temperatures, gold is a ____ and oxygen is a ____.
    a. liquid, gas
    b. gas, solid
    c. solid, gas
    d. gas, liquid

_____ 35. Dissolving salt in water forms a(n)
    a. solution
    b. gas
    c. solid
    d. emulsion

_____ 36. Air is a
    a. single compound
    b. mixture of many different gases
    c. single element
    d. none of the above

_____ 37. The freezing of water is
    a. a chemical change
    b. a physical change
    c. a nuclear change
    d. fermentation

_____ 38. When silver tarnishes, it has undergone
    a. no change whatsoever
    b. a physical change
    c. a nuclear change
    d. a chemical change

_____ 39. The French scientist who first discovered radioactivity was
    a. Urbain Leverrier
    b. Louis Pasteur
    c. Henri Becquerel
    d. Enrico Fermi

_____ 40. Mixtures of two or more metals to prevent oxidation are
    a. galvanized
    b. compounds
    c. alloys
    d. solutions

_____ 41. Rusting is an example of
    a. rapid reduction
    b. rapid oxidation
    c. slow oxidation
    d. slow reduction

_____ 42. Combustion is an example of
    a. slow oxidation
    b. rapid oxidation
    c. rapid reduction
    d. slow reduction

_____ 43. The English scientist who discovered oxygen gas was
    a. Joseph Priestly   c. Sir Isaac Newton
    b. Antoine Lavoisier   d. Urbain Leverrier

_____ 44. The French scientist who did further work with oxygen and gave it its name was
    a. Joseph Priestly   c. Sir Isaac Newton
    b. Antoine Lavoisier   d. Urbain Leverrier

_____ 45. A material that burns readily is called
    a. a conductor   c. non-combustible material
    b. inflammable material   d. combustible material

_____ 46. The gas which is necessary to support combustion is
    a. hydrogen   c. carbon monoxide
    b. oxygen   d. carbon dioxide

_____ 47. Before a combustible material can burn, it must first be changed to
    a. a solid   c. a gas
    b. a liquid   d. fuel

_____ 48. A good fuel is one that
    a. oxidizes completely   c. produces little smoke
    b. produces little soot or ash   d. all of the above

_____ 49. Fire produced when heat from chemical action raises a material to its kindling point is called
    a. spontaneous combustion   c. combustion
    b. conflagration   d. spontaneous oxidation

_____ 50. The temperature at which a combustible material starts to burn is called the
    a. burning point   c. kindling point
    b. boiling point   d. combustion point

ST. JEROME SCHOOL

Grade 7 Report Card for the _____AD-_____AD School Year

Student's Name_____

Subject	1st Quarter	2nd Quarter	3rd Quarter	4th Quarter	Final Grade
Religion					
Logic					
Spelling					
Grammar					
Reading					
History					
Math					
Science					
Music Theory					

PERCENTAGE TO LETTER GRADE CONVERSION

LETTER	A+	A	A-	B+	B	B-	C+
%	97%-100%	93-96%	90%-92%	87%-89%	83%-86%	80%-82%	77%-79%
LETTER	C	C-	D+	D	D-	F	
%	73%-76%	70%-72%	67%-69%	63%-66%	60%-62%	0%-59%	

Notes from Teacher

1st Quarter_____

2nd Quarter_____

3rd Quarter_____

4th Quarter_____

Parent's Signature _____

Map #1

Antarctica

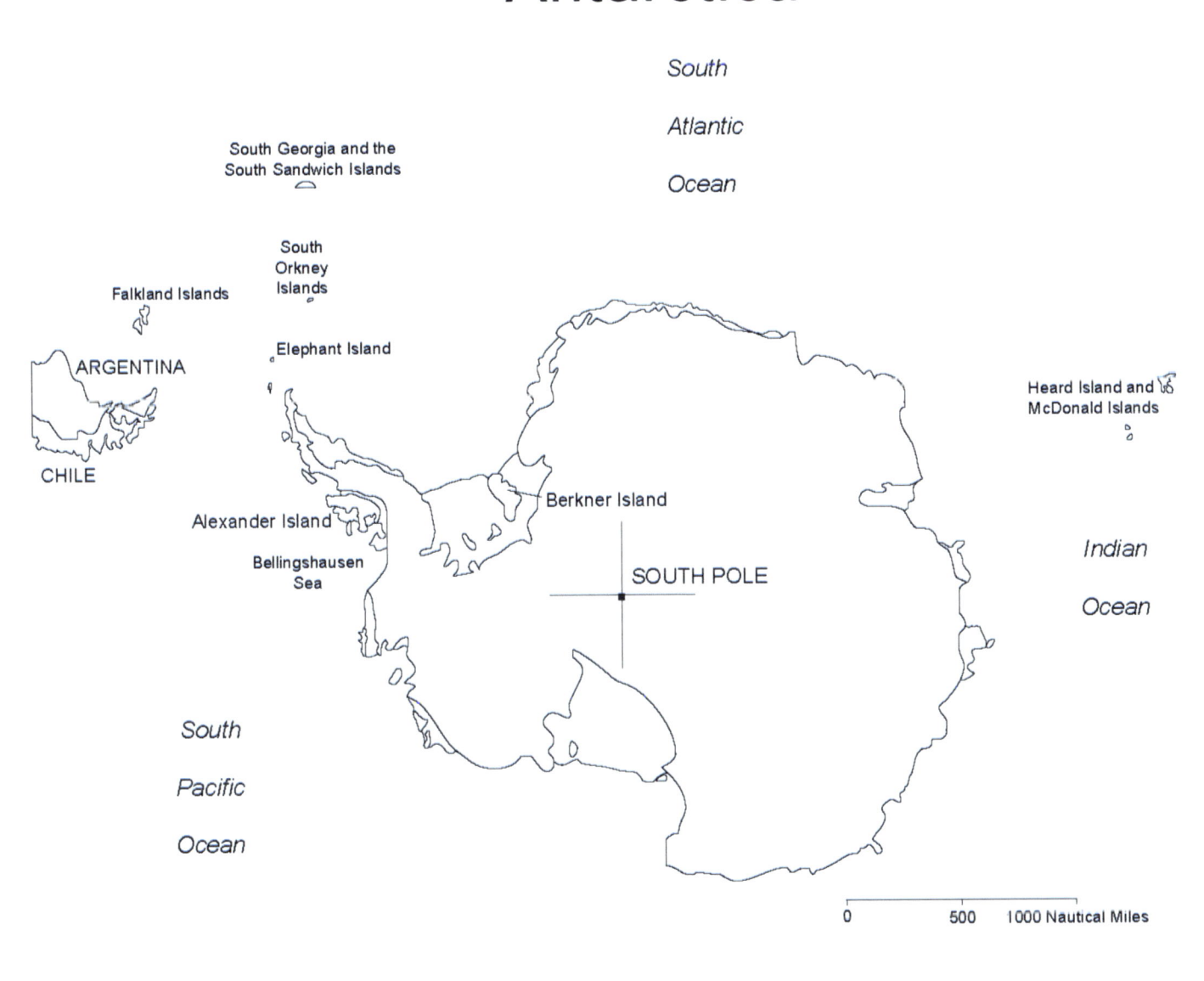

- South Atlantic Ocean
- South Georgia and the South Sandwich Islands
- South Orkney Islands
- Falkland Islands
- Elephant Island
- ARGENTINA
- CHILE
- Alexander Island
- Bellingshausen Sea
- Berkner Island
- SOUTH POLE
- Heard Island and McDonald Islands
- Indian Ocean
- South Pacific Ocean

0   500   1000 Nautical Miles

Map #2

Antarctica

Antarctica
List of Countries, Points of Interest, and Bodies of Water for Map #2

Alexander Island
Argentina
Atlantic Ocean
Bellingshausen Sea
Berkner Island
Chile
Elephant Island
Falkland Islands
Heard Island and McDonald Islands
Indian Ocean
Pacific Ocean
South Georgia and the South Sandwich Islands
South Orkney Islands
South Pole

Africa

Map #3

Africa

Map #4

Africa
List of Countries and Bodies of Water for Map #4

Algeria
Angola
Atlantic Ocean
Botswana
Chad
Egypt
Ethiopia
Indian Ocean
Kenya
Libya
Madagascar
Moroco
Mozambique
Niger
Nigeria
Somalia
South Africa
Sudan
Tanzania
Tunisia
Uganda
Zambia
Zimbabwe

SJS Book Report

Book Title:

Author:

Student Name:

Grade:

Submission Date:

Plot (what happened)

Characters

Themes (Main Idea)

Conflicts and Resolutions

Favorite event

Personal Impressions

Made in the USA
Columbia, SC
26 April 2024